AF394397

THE
COMPACT
GARDEN

THE COMPACT GARDEN

A Beginner's Guide to Growing Vegetables in Small Spaces

CHAR & MARV LOPEZ

Publisher Mike Sanders
Executive Editor Alexander Rigby
Editorial Director Ann Barton
Art & Design Director William Thomas
Designer Joanna Price
Photographers Char & Marv Lopez
Illustrator Claire Loon Baldwin
Editorial Assistant Resham Anand
Developmental Editor Tiffany Taing
Copy Editor Mira S. Park
Proofreaders Bianca Bosman, Jaye Whitney Deber
Indexer Johnna VanHoose Dinse

First American Edition, 2026
Published in the United States by DK Publishing
1745 Broadway, 20th Floor, New York, NY 10019

The authorized representative in the EEA is Dorling Kindersley
Verlag GmbH. Arnulfstr. 124, 80636 Munich, Germany

Library of Congress Number: 2025941372
ISBN 978-0-5939-6856-7

DK books are available at special discounts when purchased
in bulk for sales promotions, premiums, fundraising, or
educational use. For details, contact SpecialSales@dk.com

Printed and bound in China

www.dk.com

To our son, who we've nurtured and
watched grow with endless love
and joy. We love you always!

CONTENTS

INTRODUCTION

Hello! It's lovely to meet you. Thanks for joining us. We are Marv and Char, a husband-and-wife gardening duo from the suburbs of Toronto. You might have picked up this book after seeing us on social media, in which case you know that *The Compact Garden* is something we live with every day—literally! Our space is not very large. In fact, it's only 171 square yards (143 square meters) total, but we have managed to nurture plants from arugula to zucchini and everything in between.

Our backyard, which was once a mostly empty piece of land, has become home to garlic cloves, spinach, cabbages, and tomatoes. We enjoy fresh organic lettuce and wasabi. We've learned that leafy greens like spinach, kale, and bok choy flourish in small-space gardens, and that the same goes for herbs like cilantro, parsley, basil, and chives and vegetables such as radishes, carrots, beans, and peas. Even fruiting plants like tomatoes, peppers, cucumbers, and strawberries flourish in small spaces.

Neither of us has ever taken an agriculture or gardening course, let alone obtained a degree from a fancy school. We do not come from families of farmers, and we do not have access to special equipment or gurus who taught us everything we know. We are entirely self-taught through the painstaking but rewarding process of trial and error—though we had plenty of help from books and YouTube videos. And yet, by coming to this as amateurs and learning from the ground up, we have turned our backyard into a paradise and cultivated an amazing community of garden-lovers online. And since we did this on our own, you can, too. The only thing stopping you was that you didn't have all the tools you needed between the covers of a book. Now you do.

We became experts in compact gardening because it was our only option. We never had a vast space on which to grow something spectacular, and we still don't. But we learned how to use every inch of land—and even more importantly, how to grow vertically to take advantage of the airspace. Oftentimes, when people think of gardening, they imagine only putting things into the ground and envision acres and acres of land to make it happen. But there is far more space—endless space, in fact—above all that ground. Our backyard is living proof.

It all started for us with a patchy piece of grass in a backyard in the 'burbs. We met in college in 2002 at a graphic design program in Toronto, and in 2007, after dating for several years, we moved in with Char's mother in a suburb just north of the city called Richmond Hill.

Richmond Hill has many wonderful things going for it, but we found it to be a typical suburb without much easy access to nature. Marv became enthralled with the outdoors while growing up in the Philippines and was determined to find a way to continue enjoying the natural world when we made Richmond Hill our home.

The only way to do so was to create a garden at the house. Marv bought some simple tomato plants, cucumber seeds, and cantaloupe seedlings at Home Depot. With nothing more than a positive attitude and hope, he trekked into the backyard, dug up some grass, placed some things in the ground, and waited.

And waited . . . and waited.

We knew so little about gardening that Marv figured he could just plant some seeds—in the shaded part of the backyard, no less—and simply wait for delicious vegetables to materialize. As if it were as easy as Jack dropping magic beans into the ground and them turning into a beanstalk! Marv's grandmother had a small garden in the Philippines, but the only thing he remembers about it was eating a hot chili pepper from one of the plants. Decades later in Toronto, he failed to realize that plants need essential things to grow—like sunlight! Water! Compost!

Of course, those plants in our backyard did not bear much fruit (or anything else), and the seeds barely sprouted. Needless to say, Char's mother wasn't too impressed with her son-in-law!

But then we heard about a community garden in Aurora. Marv volunteered, and a kindly older man began teaching him the basics of how to grow plants, fruits, and vegetables. Things like how to fertilize plants, the importance of feeding soil with good compost, and ways to keep everything watered properly even on the hottest summer days. Getting educated about these matters was invigorating and inspiring. And Marv donated everything he grew there to the local food bank, giving us our first taste of the joy of sharing homegrown food.

About fifteen years later, after a stopover in a condo (more about that experience later), we moved into a different Toronto suburb, where we now have a virtual garden paradise in our backyard. Even better, our plot of delights is so overflowing that we can gift these treasures to grateful neighbors, friends, and family. Best of all, perhaps, we can share our legions of homegrown beauties with you—first online and now in the book you are holding in your hands. Our journey has taught us many things, all of which we are excited to share with you in *The Compact Garden*.

Looking back, the first and perhaps most important lesson we learned is that Marv's missteps in the backyard in 2007 weren't failures at all. Instead, they were a crucial introduction to the most critical concept in gardening: *There is no alternative to trial and error.*

Growing plants, fruits, and vegetables is a process, one that involves many moving parts. There is no way to avoid making mistakes, going wrong, or suffering disappointments along the way. But what might first appear to you as irredeemable failures are actually training exercises for future successes. By learning from our errors, we become more educated and experienced. That's the definition of progress, and learning by doing things improperly is an indispensable component of planting at home. Experimenting with new methods, trying fresh techniques, and flirting with novel technologies

Our 2016 mini garden, before we moved into the home where our garden now thrives.
We've learned to maximize our growing space, and our compact garden today is much different because of it.

are precisely what make someone a gardener. If we can inspire you to not only read this book and try it at home, but to fashion some of your own original ideas—and not be too discouraged when some of them don't quite materialize as you had first imagined—then we will have done our job.

The second insight we want to impart also comes from our own adventures. In 2009, after we'd lived with Char's mother, we moved into a condo that became our home for the next five years. It wasn't big—a one-bedroom in a high-rise building. But after the thrill and hands-on education that Marv experienced in the community gardens, he was determined to continue growing things wherever we lived, even in a concrete jungle famous for its icy winters. At the same time, Char delved into a book about self-sufficiency, which touched on the value of growing your own food. Buoyed by this combined energy, we purchased five potted plants and a mini greenhouse. The sole window in our condo faced south, and we got sunlight there only from late morning until early afternoon. And yet, even with these limitations, we grew some delicious tomatoes and leafy greens. That's how we learned it doesn't matter how small your physical space is. What matters is the size of your imagination. And *that* space is limitless.

This book is designed specifically for people with small spaces but big hopes and dreams for gardening. In *The Compact Garden*, you'll learn the basics of compact gardening: concepts, tips, and techniques that will enable you to build your own Garden of Eden wherever you live—no matter the size of your home. Live in a small apartment? No problem! As long as you have a windowsill, you can apply the methods and practices you'll learn

in *The Compact Garden* to create something lovely and delicious. The truth is, you don't need a lot of land or a lot of time to make a beautiful, bountiful garden. Our simple and easy-to-follow guide walks you through each step of planning, planting, and maintaining your own organic vegetable garden, regardless of the space or experience available.

You may be beginner gardeners who want to start with smaller-scale, low-investment gardens. Or perhaps you are a gardener in an urban area with limited growing space. Or, possibly, you simply want to grow your own food and live more sustainably. Whatever the case, if you are looking for new and fresh ways to do big things with small spaces, this book is for you. Even if you plan to one day live on an entire farm and be an expert cultivator of the land, *The Compact Garden* is still a great place to begin, because starting small is where you'll learn the quickest. The worst thing that can happen to any garden enthusiast is to get so discouraged when problems arise, as they inevitably do, that they get overwhelmed with negative feelings and give up entirely. Having a smaller space is advantageous because it gives you a more manageable place to work with, experiment in, and eventually master. From there, you can continually expand your horizons.

Here are some of the hacks, creative do-it-yourself ideas, and expert tips we'll talk about in the coming pages:

SMALL-SPACE GARDENING:
- Discover how to assess your available area and understand microclimates in the city.
- Learn how to set up raised beds, containers, and vertical gardens to maximize growing space.

- Create biodiversity in small areas using combinations of flowers, herbs, and vegetables to welcome beneficial insects.

BEGINNER-FRIENDLY VEGGIES:

- Receive guidance for selecting easy-to-grow, low-maintenance crops, including tomatoes, cucumbers, lettuce, beans, peas, and more.
- Get the 101 on how to grow delicious treats 365 days a year, regardless of the climate where you're living.
- Determine the best growth timelines and names of specific varieties of fruits and vegetables.
- Achieve dense planting of vegetable varieties to maximize containers and garden beds.

ORGANIC PRODUCE AT HOME:

- Manage pests and fertilize plants without the use of synthetic chemicals.
- Understand lighting and planting requirements.

Especially if you're a beginner, it is easy to get overwhelmed when encountering the wild world of gardening. But with our step-by-step DIY instructions, you'll be able to create a functional garden that provides fresh and healthy produce and adds beauty to your surroundings.

We taught ourselves—and now we'll teach you—how to grow hydroponically. Gardening is usually associated with the outdoors, of course. But if you know anything about Canada, you know that the winters here are cold and sometimes long, two factors that are distinctly inhospitable to cultivating fruits and vegetables. So we got into indoor gardening out of necessity, but we soon realized that growing things indoors is a luxury that

more people can and should take advantage of year-round. All you need is a kitchen countertop and some plastic containers. And gardening indoors has some unique benefits—for example, the presence of bugs can be wholly eliminated and prevented.

Before you get your hands too deep in the soil, before you go on a shopping spree and buy gear, before anything, really, ask yourself why you want to begin gardening. There are many other ways to spend your time that don't require you to get dirty, right? And we can tell you from experience that growing your own produce isn't always easy. But we can also tell you that gardening is one of the healthiest, most rewarding, and most enriching experiences you can undertake. We only regret that we didn't get started earlier.

Still not convinced? There are many wonderful reasons to start your own garden. Here are eleven of the best:

- You'll have access to fresh organic vegetables and fruits. Gifting yourself nutritious food is one of the best things you can do for yourself. Not only does it provide you with a sense of self-sufficiency, but it also promotes a healthier and more sustainable lifestyle. And food just tastes better when you grow it yourself!
- When you share the fruits of your labor with family, friends, and community, you spread this joy and nutrition to the people you love. What's more rewarding than that?
- You can cultivate your own medicinal herbal remedies.
- You are helping to reduce food waste. According to the United Nations World Food Programme, one-fifth of food produced for human consumption is lost or wasted globally—

about one billion meals a day. So when you eat what you grow, you are helping solve a major problem!

- You will learn about the natural world, develop new skills, accrue fresh knowledge about plants, the ecosystem, and their life cycles, and adapt to challenges that arise as you encounter all of this.

- You'll gain a deeper connection with nature. This was the principal draw to gardening for Marv initially, and he found his hopes realized. Sometimes, when people think of immersing themselves in nature, they imagine they need to find a forest or a national park. But anyone with a garden understands that nature can be found right at home.

- Spending time in nature has been shown to reduce stress levels and improve mental well-being.

- You'll gain training in determination and optimism. Even when things don't work out in the garden, you can rest assured there is always another season to come, which means there is always another chance to try again.

- By shortening the distance that food travels (what are called "food miles"), you are lessening your carbon footprint. The average meal travels 1,500 miles (2,500 kilometers) before it lands on your table, so getting things from your backyard or kitchen counter makes a difference!

- Gardening keeps you physically active, bending, twisting, and moving all around, so there's no need for a gym membership!

- You are creating something visually beautiful! And there can't be too much beauty in this crazy world.

We could go on! Overall, gardening is about cultivating a deeper connection to where your food comes from, sharing that joy with family, friends, and community, and embracing wholehearted and simple living. As you move through the book and embark on your own journey with soil and plants, return to these pages if you get discouraged or have doubts. Those, too, can be part of the process—which makes overcoming these obstacles as sweet as the peppers you can taste from your own efforts.

Remember: With the right resources and some practice, anyone (including you) can become a successful gardener. Enjoy the process, and don't hesitate to seek help from the gardening community. Many resources, including gardening books like this one and online tutorials, are available for beginners—check out our social media pages for suggestions if you haven't yet. Consider joining a local gardening club, which can provide support and knowledge from experienced gardeners.

Get ready to embark on a rewarding journey of growing your own organic vegetables with *The Compact Garden*. Let's get sprouting!

GETTING STARTED

The world is a big place. Sometimes, it can seem too big, especially if you're trying to change parts of it, and it might be difficult to know where to start. As much as we want to see you growing a flourishing *Jumanji*-level jungle right away—and you probably want that, too—we don't want you to take on more than you can handle and end up feeling overwhelmed and discouraged before you even begin.

For that reason, we recommend you start small. Think about setting up a manageable little garden first, perhaps in a patch of grass in your front yard or something potted in your home. Starting with pots or small containers can be a much more manageable learning method. You can pick a few plants and grow what you eat. Experiment with watering those plants consistently and watch them grow. As time goes on, you'll gain experience and confidence through trial and error, you'll learn to expand your garden space, and you'll be forced to be creative with your available space, taking advantage of every square inch and, hopefully, discovering the magic of vertical gardening.

When we moved into our current home in 2019, our backyard garden was about 80 percent grass and filled with cherry, apple, pear, peach, and plum trees the previous owner had planted and left behind. There were also three black currant berry shrubs. At the time, we were growing one zucchini plant, a pepper, potatoes, and tomatoes. As relative beginners, we didn't think much about building a compact garden—digging a new garden bed simply wasn't on our minds yet. We started very small, creating a 3x3-foot garlic patch, plus four planters that were each 2x3 feet. The great thing about planters is that they are portable, which allowed us to discern which areas were best suited for growing and enabled us to manage a small garden without getting overwhelmed. Success!

That being said, the reality is that you're probably going to start with whatever is available to you. You might be living on or near a farm with acres of land at your disposal. We completely understand if you want to go big or go home. If that's the case, then go for it! We'll be your cheerleaders. And our advice throughout this book still works for you, too.

The point is to get started, wherever you are, with whatever space you have at hand.

Our favorite harvest—Wiri Wiri peppers. These small Guyanese gems pack serious heat and incredible flavor.

Maximize small spaces through strategic canopy design, so each plant layer gets its share of sunlight.

ASSESSING YOUR AVAILABLE AREA

Site selection is essential when you start planning your garden. Most crops grow best in full sun, which is defined as 6 hours of direct sunlight a day. So, aim for the sunniest spots you have, unless you live in some sort of desert, in which case you'll want to opt for shadier spots.

Notice that we said crops grow *best* in full sun. However, they can manage in darker spots as well. Imagine a typical forested area: Big canopy trees cover plants, and big plants cover small ones. Even in this multilayered environment, plants thrive. This principle applies in your home garden, too. Different plants have different light requirements; some flourish in full sun, while others prefer shade. Still other plants can thrive under partial shade *and* full shade. It's about finding the right plants to grow in each part of your garden.

We figured out this concept by accident—a common theme for us. By 2022, our garden had expanded, and we became hooked on growing more food (you'll probably develop this addiction yourself soon enough). We built several raised garden beds and started putting them in shaded and semi-shaded spots. Initially, we didn't know which plants were best suited for shady locations.

We tried vegetables like cucumbers, sweet potatoes, potatoes, eggplants, tomatoes, and peppers. Most suffered stunted growth due to lack of sun, although the eggplants and peppers still managed to fruit. Ever since, we've been trying different varieties in shaded areas, testing which vegetables will grow without direct sunlight. We also started implementing techniques such as canopy growing. For example, we planted a tomato that grew tall, then planted low-growing and shade-tolerant plants, like celery, beside it. For this to work, we had to stake our tomato plant and prune the bottom leaves as it grew, allowing light to pass through to the lower area. By doing this, the celery received ample light for it to grow healthily. Some vegetables, like people, just go well together.

Experimentation is one of the most rewarding, intellectually challenging, and downright fun aspects of gardening. People don't mention it much because it sometimes involves failure, but the process itself is more than enough reward, even when the results fall short of what we desire. And, of course, the chance of failure makes the eventual success all the more rewarding.

THE IMPORTANCE OF WATER

When choosing your garden location, you'll want to select a space close to a water source. Lugging bowls or containers full of H_2O back and forth from your tap to your plants becomes exhausting and sometimes painful if you have to do it hundreds of times. And if you have a physical disability, transporting that water might not be possible at all. So, the closer to water you are, the better. For a lot of people in developed countries, a primary water source is a tap you can attach a hose to that funnels water provided by your municipality.

Catching rainwater is usually the next best option. In fact, it's the first best option in compact gardens, because besides conserving a vital resource, rainwater makes your plants happy. They like rainwater best, as it contains nitrates and washed-off dust and is pure hydration, devoid of any chemicals found in municipal water. Tap water is usually more convenient and plentiful in the hot summer months, but we like to use two rain barrels to collect rainwater from the downspout of our roof. If we had more rain barrels or lived in an apartment with a balcony, we'd rely more on rainwater. If you have a bigger budget and a larger garden, one of the best ways to collect rainwater is a rainwater tank, which also filters the collected water.

Capturing nature's gift: Our rain barrel system keeps the garden hydrated sustainably.

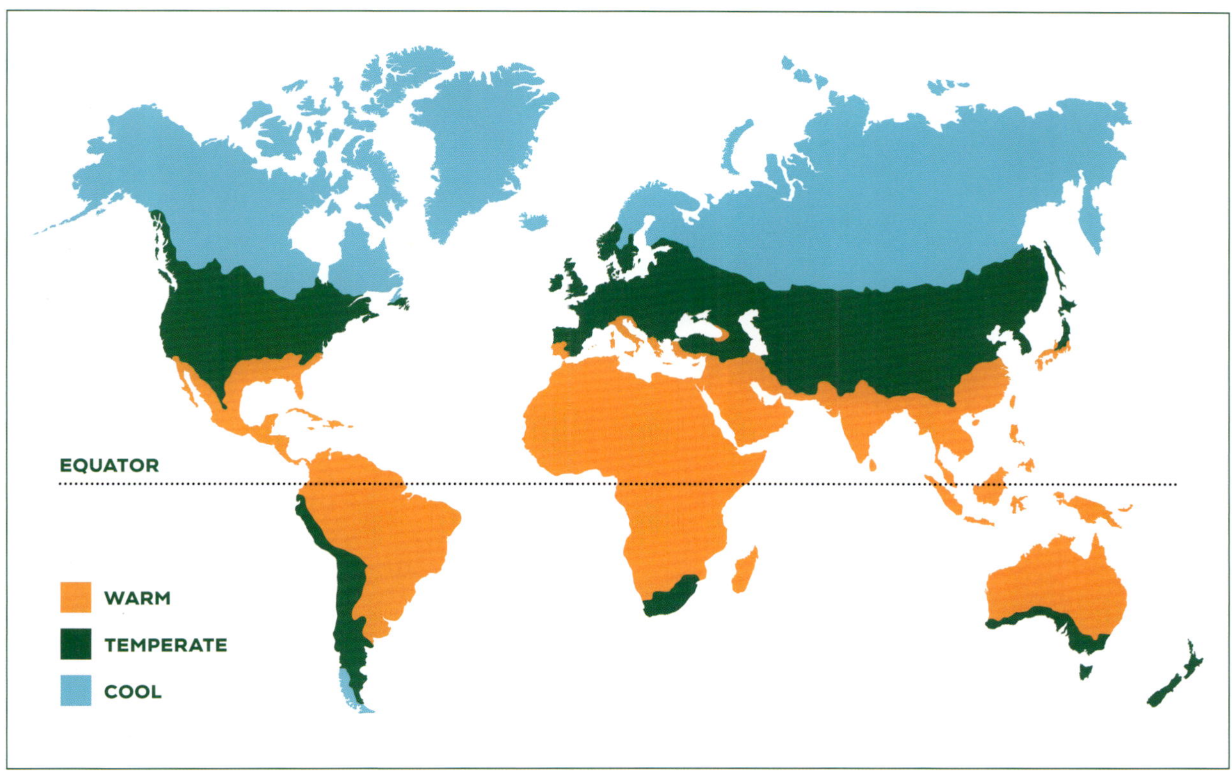

GETTING TO KNOW YOUR CLIMATE

When starting your garden, understanding the kind of climate you're in will help you choose the right plants to thrive in your backyard. There are three main types of climates: warm, temperate, and cool. Each comes with its own distinctive personality.

Warm climates: If you live in a warm climate, you enjoy long, hot summers and mild winters. These areas hardly see frost, making them perfect for growing sun-loving plants. Think of places like Florida, Brazil, and Southeast Asia. In these regions, you can grow vegetables like tomatoes, peppers, and eggplants almost all year round.

Temperate climates: In temperate areas, you experience four distinct seasons, meaning you get to enjoy warm summers and cooler winters. Think of places like the UK, Switzerland, and the Pacific Northwest in the US. Here, you can grow a variety of crops throughout the year.

Cool climates: If you're in a cool climate like us, you'll notice that winters are cold and summers are short but warm. This means you'll have to be a bit more strategic about what and when you plant. Think of parts of Canada, Scandinavia, and the northern US. In these areas, gardening can be a bit of a challenge, but with the right planning, you can still grow plenty of delicious food.

MICROCLIMATES IN THE CITY

You may have heard the term "season extenders"—tools or techniques used to prolong the growing season by protecting plants from adverse weather conditions. Greenhouses are the best season extenders, but row covers, bed covers, and even plastic bottles fit the bill. Recycled plastic bottles can be used as mini greenhouses for individual plants or small groups of seedlings by cutting the bottom off and placing the bottle over a plant to protect your little babies from the elements.

In September 2021, we built a permanent cover for our raised bed, made of 6-mil polyethylene plastic. Our expectation was that we'd be able to grow lettuce, kale, and spinach all winter long. We knew there were limited choices of plants that could withstand colder temperatures. The cover turned out great, protecting the vegetables from freezing weather—at first. We assumed our setup was enough to grow vegetables even on the coldest winter days. But the plants lasted only through December, and by the time the temperature dropped below 32°F/0°C (aka the freezing point of water), there wasn't much happening. The plants were surviving but not growing and had gone dormant and sad. Our hope of harvesting in the middle of winter had failed. On the positive side, we found the cover useful because it at least extended our growing season all the way to December—most plants of ours usually died by the end of October. The cover also enabled us to plant earlier in April because the soil thaws much faster beneath it.

That's how it works here in the compact garden: You win some; you lose some. But your losses are victories in disguise.

Our covered raised beds help us get a jump on the growing season and protect plants from frosts and pests.

PLANNING A COMPACT GARDEN

Congratulations! You have decided to start gardening and have assessed your available area to determine what might work best. It's time to consider the ideal growing style to meet your needs. There are different ways of structuring a garden, including ours. Each design has its pros and cons, so it's good to understand the respective strengths and weaknesses up front. We use all three methods, in different places, in fact, because they all offer something different. Now, let's dig in—pun intended!

CHOOSING THE RIGHT GROWING STYLE

IN-GROUND

When people think of gardening, they usually think of in-ground. This method involves planting directly into the native soil of a garden plot, utilizing the existing soil structure and nutrients and allowing plants to grow in their natural environment. For as long as humans have been around, we have been gardening in-ground.

INDOOR

We opt for indoor gardening when the weather gets cold here in Ontario, but some people may want to always grow in a sheltered space, which we'll discuss in more detail in Chapter 7. While it is more expensive—you must pay more for lighting, for instance—growing inside offers some advantages. Namely, you can avoid bugs, gophers, squirrels, and other unwanted creatures, and you don't have to stop working when the sun goes down.

RAISED BEDS

Raised beds elevate the growing area above ground level, improving drainage and soil quality while reducing weed competition. Raised beds allow for better access when planting and harvesting and help to avoid compacting the soil underneath, enabling better control of the soil conditions.

Winter gardening inside the house, keeping the harvest going year-round.

Why We Like Raised Beds

Raised bed gardening has become more popular these days—most likely because of the increased demand for readily available fresh produce. One of the biggest reasons we choose to grow in raised beds versus in direct soil is because our yard backs into a ravine with several tall black walnut trees close to our fence. All parts of the black walnut tree, including its roots, leaves, and nuts, contain a chemical compound called juglone, which acts as a respiratory inhibitor for many plants, leading to symptoms such as wilting, yellowing leaves, and stunted growth. Essentially, it strangles plants. The most common garden vegetables, including tomatoes, potatoes, and peppers, are particularly sensitive to juglone and fare poorly near black walnut trees. Raised beds prevent the walnut trees from causing trouble!

Shovel
Hand Rake
Stick
Gardening Gloves
Ruler
Plant Hole Digger
Hori Hori Knife
Shears
Hand Shovel
Dibbler
Hand Fork
Twine

CONTAINER GARDENING

GROW BAGS

Grow bags are lightweight and made from breathable, durable fabrics that allow for proper air circulation and drainage, both of which are fundamental for healthy root development. Our garden has a section composed entirely of grow bags and containers. Grow bags do well with drip irrigation, even on extremely hot days. Our grow-bag-container soil mix is filled with equal parts coco coir or peat, perlite or vermiculite, and finished compost. We also add a handful of fertilizer every 2 weeks.

Fabric grow bags provide superior aeration and prevent root circling, creating stronger plants in our compact space.

POTS

You can still grow vegetables and fruits in containers when you have no usable outdoor garden space, as pots can be placed on balconies, patios, and windowsills. Growing in pots also gives you complete control over the soil quality, since you can quickly move containers to take advantage of sunlight or protect plants from extreme weather conditions. Container gardening also reduces the risk of pests and diseases. (Tip: Eggplant grows particularly well in containers. You can even plant them in steps and create a stair garden, as we did.)

The downside of pot-based gardening is that plants need to be watered more and regularly fed with fertilizer. You also must be careful about choosing the right size pot. Among our biggest gardening mistakes was growing a cherry tomato in a 3-gallon pot. With so little room to grow, the tomato was stunted and barely reached full size. The roots had no room to spread, and the fruits were nowhere to be seen. Even though we watered our tomato plant consistently, fed it with fertilizer monthly, and ensured it had access to full sun, it wasn't enough! The pot would have been more than adequate if we were growing a micro dwarf tomato, such as an orange hat. But for a cherry or indeterminate tomato variety, a 5- to 10-gallon pot would have been a much better choice to provide enough space for the roots to expand and access nutrients.

VERTICAL GARDENING TECHNIQUES

Vertical gardening is one of the most successful methods we've used in our garden, allowing us to fully utilize all corners of our garden with the help of trellises, stakes, arches, and walls. Growing vertically allows plants in shaded spots to reach more sunlight when they grow tall enough, eventually. We have installed small planters on our fence walls to grow micro dwarf vegetables and herbs and created a unique garden bed that features a vertical wall with several small planters built into it. By applying vertical gardening techniques, we've more than doubled our growing space. For those just starting out, we recommend using a trellis—a frame of crossed bars that supports plants as they grow.

STAKES

Despite what you may have learned from watching old horror movies, stakes are not primarily used to kill vampires. Driving stakes into the soil next to plants helps provide support as they grow. We find this particularly effective for indeterminate varieties of tomatoes and peppers. (Tip: If you ever grow sunflowers, keep the stalks and dry them. They make great trellises and free stakes to support tall plants.)

LATTICE PANELS

Lattice panels can be attached to walls or fences, serving as versatile supports for climbing vegetables. Elevating plants with lattice panels enhances airflow around the foliage, which can reduce humidity levels and minimize the risk of fungal diseases, promoting healthier plant growth. Vegetables growing on a lattice allow for easier access for maintenance tasks like pruning and harvesting. Lattice panels can be used in various configurations and styles, making them adaptable to different garden designs. They can also serve multiple purposes in addition to supporting plants, such as a privacy screen or a decorative feature.

Vertical zucchini: Training stems upward with stakes saves precious ground space.

Our narrow trellis system:
perfect for peas in tight spaces
while keeping the pathway clear.

When space is limited, think vertical!

Building upward with purpose—custom
trellis frameworks turn a small space into
a highly productive garden.

Our current backyard garden layout maximizes our 171-square-yard (143-square-meter) space.

GARDEN ARCHES

Garden arches are visually appealing structures that allow and support climbing plants to grow upward rather than along the ground, providing better sunlight exposure and maximizing space so you can cultivate more plants in a smaller area. Also, garden arches make harvesting easier, since the fruits can be easily reached without bending down or navigating through dense foliage.

CAGES

Caging is used for heavier crops that may be too weighty for a trellis or stake. Typically, cages are made of wire or metal and support plants as they grow. This method is particularly common for vegetables that benefit from additional support to keep their stems upright, like tomatoes, peppers, and cucumbers. Cages also promote better air circulation around the plants.

BAMBOO TEEPEE TRELLIS

A bamboo teepee trellis is a garden structure that supports climbing plants and vining crops. Typically made from long, thin bamboo poles arranged in a teepee shape, bamboo teepee trellises provide a sturdy support system for plants like pole beans, peas, and cucumbers.

STRING TRELLIS

String trellises involve hanging strings from a horizontal bar, creating a simple support system for crops like tomatoes. Twine is versatile and inexpensive, making it ideal for the beginner garden. Jute is a good choice, but we went with 100 percent cotton butcher twine for our trellis, a natural, stronger, and biodegradable option. You can also use this method in the kitchen.

WALL GARDEN AND VERTICAL PLANTERS

A wall garden involves stacked pots or containers mounted onto a wall or fence to maximize space in small areas. This allows you to grow herbs, flowers, and even some dwarf vegetables vertically.

Fence-Growing: A Step-By-Step Guide

Last year, we grew our micro-dwarf tomatoes on our fence. They were so successful that we're doing the same thing again. Here's how we did it:

STEP 1 - ATTACH FENCE BOARDS: Start by measuring and cutting your fence boards to 32 inches in length. Position the first board horizontally against the existing fence, then secure it with 3 screws. Repeat this process for the remaining 2 boards, using a total of 3 boards and 9 screws overall.

STEP 2 - INSTALL GEAR CLAMPS: Attach three 6-inch gear clamps to each fence board you just installed, using a total of 9 gear clamps for the 3 boards. These clamps will hold the pots securely in place.

STEP 3 - ADD POTS: Use one-gallon FHD square pots measuring 4.75 × 4.75 × 8 inches. These pots are narrow in width but deep in height, making them ideal for small-growing plants. Secure each pot using the gear clamps.

STEP 4 - SELECT PLANTS: Look for small-growing plants, such as herbs and micro-dwarf varieties. Red Robin tomatoes are an excellent choice, growing to about one foot tall and producing abundant cherry tomatoes.

STEP 5 - WATER CONSISTENTLY: Water the plants consistently, keeping in mind that smaller pots tend to dry out more quickly. Watering every other day is necessary unless there is substantial daily rainfall. Consider setting up drip irrigation from the top, allowing excess water to trickle down and nourish the plants below.

SOIL AND NUTRITION

Folks often think of plants as synonymous with gardening. And certainly, growing fruits, vegetables, and all other beautiful green things and enjoying the products of your hard work can be deeply gratifying. But the essence of gardening is the *soil*—it literally grounds you and houses all that we grow. That's why the words "soil" and "earth" are used interchangeably, because both are the very basis of our planet. As gardeners, you will be spending much of your time darkening your hands (or gloves) in the soil, so it behooves you to understand just what lies between your fingers.

UNDERSTANDING SOIL TYPES

LOAMY SOIL

A perfect mix of sand, silt, and clay, loamy soil is an all-you-can-eat buffet for plants that is full of nutrients, holds water well, and drains easily so roots don't drown. It's best for almost all vegetables! Think tomatoes, peppers, beans, and more. Loamy soil feels soft and crumbly in your hands, like moist chocolate cake.

SANDY SOIL

With large particles that drain water swiftly, sandy soil dries out quickly and doesn't hold nutrients well, so you'll need to water and fertilize more often. It's best for root veggies like carrots, radishes, and potatoes, which love loose soil. Sandy soil feels gritty, like beach sand, and falls apart easily.

CLAY SOIL

With tiny, tightly packed particles, clay soil holds water too well, which can suffocate plant roots, and is hard to dig when dry. It's best for veggies like broccoli and cabbage, but only if you mix it with compost to loosen it up. Clay soil feels sticky when wet and hard as a rock when dry.

SILTY SOIL

With fine particles, silty soil holds water better than sandy soil and is fertile, but it can get compacted over time. It's best for leafy greens like spinach, lettuce, and kale. Silty soil feels silky or powdery when dry and slippery when wet and is smoother than sandy soil but not as dense as clay.

PEATY SOIL

Rich in organic matter, peaty soil holds a lot of water and is usually acidic, so the pH may need to be adjusted with lime for some veggies. It's best for moisture-loving plants like celery and onions. Peaty soil is dark, feels like a wet sponge, and is often found in boggy areas.

CHALKY SOIL

Stony and alkaline (meaning having a high pH), chalky soil is not great for acid-loving plants and often lacks nutrients. It's best for veggies like cabbage, cauliflower, and other brassicas that don't mind alkaline soil. Chalky soil feels dry and stony, and water drains quickly through it.

ORGANIC SOIL

Enriched with compost, manure, or other organic materials, organic soil is packed with nutrients and supports healthy plant growth. It's best for all vegetables and is like giving your plants a multivitamin. Organic soil is rich and dark, and smells earthy.

Soil with a loose texture that's rich in nutrients helps roots establish quickly.

Before anything grows aboveground, it starts below with quality soil, which is the key to consistent seed germination.

Take it from us: A thriving garden needs good soil structure. When we started, we had zero understanding of (among other things) how important it is to have healthy soil in which to grow food. We simply dug up some grass at Char's mother's home and used the existing soil underneath it. And why not? The earth was right there for us! Thinking that the soil offered enough fertile ground for what we were planting, we didn't add anything else—no vitamins or minerals. Looking back, we know we should have at least added compost to improve the soil. Well, in the end, we were correct in thinking that we could grow something with that soil, but we were wrong about the plant growing big and strong enough to fruit! What we got instead was a plant that didn't offer any of the goodies we'd anticipated. It was, quite literally, fruitless.

Persistent people that we are, this setback didn't stop us. Instead, we picked up an excellent book called *Square Foot Gardening* by Mel Bartholomew. He described his soil mix as equal parts vermiculite, peat moss, and organic blended compost. He didn't just rely on whatever was in

the ground in front of him. This was a revelation for us! It was the first time we understood that good soil structure is what makes the whole shebang work. Just as having the right colors is essential to a painter and playing the correct instrument is necessary for a musician, so, too, is having right soil mixture in the art of gardening.

Ever since, we've been applying Mel's mix throughout our garden, from containers to raised beds. We made one alteration, however. Instead of using vermiculite, which retains moisture, we switched it with perlite, which helps loosen the soil and improves drainage. If peat moss isn't ethically ideal for you—its extraction releases carbon and contributes to a warming climate— coco coir, which is environmentally sustainable and holds a lot of water, is a good replacement. For compost, we eventually started making our own simply by composting organic materials from the kitchen and our garden. By adjusting our soil structure, we've been able to grow healthier, more productive plants. And it didn't stop there—we are always looking for ways to improve the health of our garden soil as part of our ongoing journey.

SOIL FOR BEDS

Since compact gardening harnesses the power of raised beds and cont-ainers, you must know which soil is best. First, it's good to understand the typical soil mixes you can purchase from big-box stores. Vegetable potting mixes are typically soil-less blends designed to balance moisture retention, aeration, and nutrients for container-grown vegetables. Here's a breakdown of the average ingredients commonly found in these mixes:

Base material (70%)	**Sphagnum peat moss or coconut coir (coir fiber):** Used for their moisture retention and lightweight structure.
Aeration materials (10 to 20%)	**Perlite:** A lightweight volcanic material that improves drainage and aeration. **Vermiculite:** Helps retain moisture and nutrients while also improving aeration.
Organic matter (optional)	**Compost or worm castings:** Adds nutrients and supports beneficial microbes for plant growth.
Fertilizers	**Slow-release fertilizers:** Often included to provide essential nutrients over time. **Dolomite lime:** Sometimes added to balance the pH, especially if peat moss is used (as it can be acidic).
Other Additives	**Sand or bark:** Occasionally added for additional drainage and structure, depending on the specific needs of the vegetables.

Container vs. Ground Soil

Avoid using regular garden soil in containers, as it tends to compact and restrict airflow to the roots. Container mixes should be lighter and fluffier, incorporating materials like perlite or coconut coir. Ground beds, on the other hand, can handle denser mixes that include more native soil.

HOMEMADE SOIL MIXES

Don't limit yourself to purchasing premade mixes, because you can start mixing your own organic garden soil. Throughout our gardening journey, we have always worked to improve our soil blend, trying different mixes to see what works best. We encourage you to experiment as well.

Here are a few sample mixes we made for garden beds and containers.

TRIPLE MIX

Triple mix soil is a blend of three main ingredients: topsoil, peat moss, and compost, mixed in equal parts. This mix is excellent for gardens because it improves poor soil, making it easier for plants to grow healthy and strong. The topsoil provides structure and minerals, the peat moss helps retain moisture and keeps the soil light, and the compost adds nutrients and organic matter to feed the plants.

SUPERFOOD SOIL MIX

This blend is what we've been using in our garden bed. It consists of three main ingredients mixed in equal parts: coco coir, perlite, and compost. This mix is great for raised garden beds or containers because it feeds your plants and retains moisture while allowing for good drainage and aeration to keep them healthy. We like to use coco coir because it holds water well and drains better than peat moss. Perlite improves drainage and keeps the soil light and airy, giving the plant roots enough oxygen. And compost is like a superfood for your soil, improving its structure, fertility, and overall health.

CONTAINER AND GROW-BAG MIX

This blend is our usual go-to for containers and consists of the following ingredients: coco coir, vermiculite, compost, worm castings, and chicken manure granules. Since containers and grow bags are compact, the soil in them tends to dry up much faster. This blend allows for moisture to stay longer. Additionally, if you're in a dry area, topping off with mulch will help prevent moisture from evaporating faster. There are two main parts to this mix:

- **Part one (80%)** is equal parts coco coir (or peat moss), vermiculite (or perlite), and compost. The coco coir and vermiculite both hold water well, with the latter helping to retain nutrients and releasing them (and water) slowly to the plants, while the compost improves the soil structure in containers.

- **Part two (20%)** is equal parts worm castings and organic chicken manure granules. Worm castings are an incredible natural fertilizer and soil enhancer, whereas organic chicken manure granules are a great natural slow-release fertilizer.

TIP: When filling containers or raised beds, fill the bottom half with materials readily available in your own home instead of using only soil, which can be costly. For instance, when Marv was packing a 17-inch raised bed once, he used cardboard and other paper materials. On top of that, he put a second layer of twigs, logs, and branches and added a third layer of unfinished compost, which still had green leaves. He placed a fourth layer of brown leaves on top of all that. By then, the container was half full, and only then did Marv put the organic soil mix as the fifth layer. He topped it with three inches of combined finished compost and perlite. In that raised bed, we grew bok choy, lettuce, and spinach, and it worked as well as if we had used soil in the entire container—except that we were also able to recycle materials that were going unused (always a good thing), saved a bunch of money, and avoided some trips to Home Depot!

SOIL TEST

If you haven't done a soil test yet, you might want to try it, preferably in the autumn, at the end of the gardening season. It's good to know exactly what's in your soil so you can determine which type of plant will thrive in it and how to amend the soil. For example, root vegetables prefer low-nitrogen soil that is higher in phosphorus, which encourages root development. Armed with that sort of knowledge, you can match the plant best suited to the soil you have.

Conducting a homemade test will enable you to understand what soil you have, but you won't be able to discern anything more in detail. For that, we suggest purchasing a soil kit. You don't need anything fancy—a simple testing kit purchased online or at any gardening store can help you determine your soil's pH (potential hydrogen) level, which can be alternately acidic (sour), neutral, or alkaline (sweet). The ideal soil pH levels vary by plant, but for the most part, you want to keep your soil pH within this range: Most vegetable garden plants grow best in acidic to near neutral conditions (5.5 to 7.5 pH). When soil pH is too high, it can pose problems for plant health and growth. For many plants, soil that is high in alkalinity makes it harder to absorb nutrients from the soil, limiting their optimal growth.

REJUVENATING SOIL HEALTH

People often ask what happens at the end of the growing season. Do we throw away all the soil in the pots and start again? Do we dig up and till our raised beds and pull all our plants? Our resounding answer: No! That would be an enormous waste of energy and resources, requiring us to unnecessarily duplicate our efforts and spend much more money. We love gardening, but not so much that we want to do twice the work for the same result!

Here's how we preserve our work. First, we limit the disturbance in whatever area we are growing. It doesn't matter if it's in pots, grow bags, direct ground, or raised beds—the less we dig, the better. Instead of digging, we add organic materials on top, just like how it would be in nature. Instead of pulling our plants, we chop the leaves and stems, leaving the roots in the ground, where they will decompose and create good drainage. The only thing that should be discarded at the end of the season are plants showing signs of disease. Everything else can stay.

Remember: Our goal is to have well-drained, nutrient-rich soil that contains living creatures—just like in the natural world. That's why, in our garden, we try to replicate what nature does. For instance, in a forest environment, leaves fall to the ground in the autumn, giving nature the organic fertilizer it needs to grow: As those leaves decompose, nutrients and organic matter are released back into the soil, broken down by insects, fungi, and microorganisms. This then leads to the formation of a rich layer of organic matter known as humus.

Well, leaves fall from trees in our backyard, too, mainly from the maple and cherry trees that are abundant where we live. We collect these fallen leaves, which become a natural fertilizer freely available even here in the suburbs. Each autumn, Marv gathers the dry leaves and places them in our raised beds. We sometimes chop the leaves down to smaller bits to make the decomposition process faster. We add those leaves on top of the fresh green leaves from the garden, which forms the bottom layer. And then on top of both materials, we add organic compost that is full of microbes. This practice allows beneficial organisms like earthworms and mycorrhizal fungi to thrive, leading to healthier soil, with improved soil structure, enhanced moisture retention, and essential nutrients for plants. We repeat this process yearly at the end of our gardening season, creating a continuous soil-building process. Over time, the soil becomes ever more fertile.

That's just one example. Elsewhere in the garden, we add other types of compost, well-rotted manure, shredded leaves, leaf mold, and other decomposed plant materials. This simple method helps improve the health of our soil year after year. Organic matter generally enhances soil structure, increases nutrients, and promotes microbial activity. It is your friend. So use whatever is naturally around you to keep your soil healthy and strong!

Building soil the way nature does: leaves and organic matter break down over time, enriching the bed for next season.

MAKING COMPOST

Composting is a way to recycle food scraps and yard waste into rich soil, which is great for your garden. There are two main types of materials: brown and green. Brown materials are high in carbon and typically dry. They include items like cardboard, wood chips, sawdust, dried leaves, twigs, and hay or straw. Green materials are high in nitrogen and are usually wet and fresh. These include fruit and vegetable scraps, manure, fresh plant material, weeds, and coffee grounds. It's ideal to use equal amounts of both brown and green materials when making compost. Avoid adding meat, dairy, and oil.

1. Gather your brown and green materials.
2. Spread a layer of one type of material on the bottom of your compost bin.
3. Add a second layer of a different type of material.
4. Add an activator, such as manure, to speed up the composting process.
5. If your compost pile is open to the air, cover it with cardboard to help keep it moist.

Understanding NPK

NPK stands for nitrogen (N), phosphorus (P), and potassium (K). These three nutrients are important for all plants to grow well and produce healthy fruits and flowers. In addition to NPK, plants also need smaller amounts of other nutrients, like calcium and magnesium.

Nitrogen is essential for plant growth. It helps make leaves green and supports strong stem development. Good sources of nitrogen include blood meal, bone meal, fish emulsion, and chicken manure granules.

Phosphorus is crucial for strong root growth. It is especially important for the development of flowers and fruits. Some examples of phosphorus sources are bone meal and rock phosphate.

Potassium, also known as potash, is vital for overall plant health. It strengthens plants, improves their ability to use water, and helps them resist diseases. You can find potassium in sources like compost, kelp, and greensand.

ORGANIC FERTILIZERS AND AMENDMENTS

Nature produces many types of fertilizers that you can use for your gardening. Here are the most common ones.

CHICKEN MANURE GRANULES

Chicken manure granules are little pellets of plant food made from chicken poop. They're dried and processed, so they don't smell as bad as you might think, and they are easy to sprinkle around your plants. These granules are packed with nutrients, especially nitrogen and calcium, that help plants grow big and green. They also release nutrients slowly, so your plants get fed over time without being overfed all at once.

WORM CASTINGS

Worm castings are basically worm poop, but don't let that gross you out! They're like magic for your garden. Worms eat organic stuff, like food scraps, and turn it into nutrient-rich soil. So worm castings are full of good stuff that helps plants grow and keeps the soil healthy. They're gentle, so you can use them on any plant without harming them.

MANURE

Manure is probably something you are familiar with. It's animal poop, usually from cows, horses, or chickens, that's been aged or composted. It's a natural fertilizer that adds nutrients and organic matter to the soil. Fresh manure can be too strong and might burn plants, so it's best to let it break down before use. Manure is excellent for improving soil health and feeding your plants.

COMPOST

Compost is like black gold for gardeners, made by letting kitchen scraps, garden waste, and other organic materials break down into rich, crumbly soil. Compost improves your soil's texture, helps it hold water, and provides a balanced mix of nutrients for your plants. Plus, it's free if you make it yourself!

BLOOD MEAL

Blood meal is dried animal blood, usually from cows or pigs, that's turned into a powder. It's super high in nitrogen, which helps plants grow lots of green leaves, and is great for leafy veggies like lettuce or spinach—but don't use too much or you might overfeed your plants.

BONE MEAL

Bone meal is made from ground up animal bones. It's rich in phosphorus and calcium, which are great for strong roots and flowers. Bone meal is perfect for bulbs, flowers, and fruiting plants. When planting, sprinkle it in the soil, and it will slowly release nutrients.

SEAWEED

Seaweed is like a multivitamin for your plants, full of trace minerals, natural growth hormones, and other goodies that help plants grow strong and healthy. You can use it fresh, dried, or as a liquid fertilizer. It's especially good for boosting plants' resilience to stress, like drought or pests.

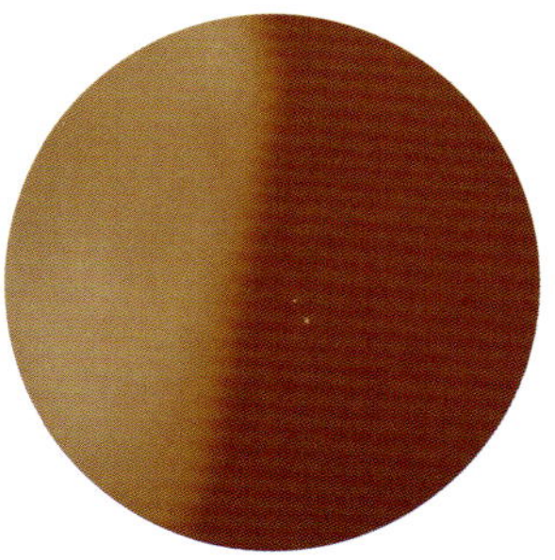

FISH EMULSION

Fish emulsion is a liquid fertilizer made from fish scraps and is high in nitrogen and other nutrients, making it great for leafy plants. It's also fast-acting and can be used as a soil drench or sprayed on leaves. Just be warned: It can smell a bit fishy!

ROCK MINERALS

Rock minerals, like basalt or granite dust, are ground up rocks that add trace elements to your soil. These minerals help plants grow better and improve soil health over time. They're especially useful if your soil is missing key nutrients.

EPSOM SALT

Epsom salt isn't the same as table salt—it's magnesium sulfate, which is great for plants that need a magnesium boost, like tomatoes, peppers, and roses. If your plant's leaves turn yellow be-tween the veins, it might need magnesium. Just dissolve some Epsom salt in water and pour it on the soil or spray it on the leaves.

GYPSUM

Gypsum is a soil amendment that adds calcium and sulfur without changing the soil's pH. It's great for breaking up heavy clay soils and improving drainage. If your soil is compacted or salty, gypsum can help fix it.

GARDEN LIME

Garden lime raises the pH of acidic soils, making them more neutral. It also adds calcium and magnesium, which are suitable for plants. If your soil is too acidic, lime can help balance it out so your plants can more easily absorb nutrients.

LEAF MOLD

Leaf mold is what you get when leaves break down into a soft, crumbly material. It's not as nutrient-rich as compost, but it's amazing for improving soil structure and water retention. Leaf mold is perfect for mulching or mixing into your garden beds.

BIOCHAR

Biochar, a type of charcoal made from burning organic material in low oxygen, is excellent for improving soil health because it holds onto nutrients and water while creating a home for beneficial microbes. Mix it into your soil to make it more fertile and long-lasting.

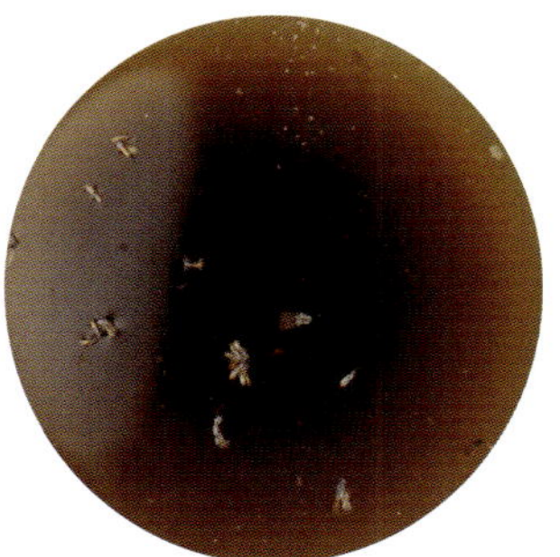

HOMEMADE LIQUID FERTILIZERS

Homemade liquid fertilizers are easy to make and super cheap. You can steep compost, worm castings, weeds, or even banana peels in water to create a nutrient-rich tea for your plants. These DIY fertilizers are a great way to recycle kitchen and garden waste while giving your plants a natural boost.

PEAT MOSS

Peat moss is a natural material harvested from bogs. It's lightweight and holds water like a sponge, helping to keep the soil moist and providing a soft, fluffy texture for plant roots to grow easily. However, it can be acidic, so lime can be added to balance the pH.

COCO COIR

Coco coir is made from the fibers of coconut husks and is a sustainable alternative to peat moss. Coco coir holds water well, like peat, but drains better, so roots don't get waterlogged. Plus, it's eco-friendly. It often comes in compressed bricks that must be soaked in water to expand before use.

PERLITE

Perlite is a type of volcanic rock that's heated until it "pops" like popcorn. In potting mixes, it looks like tiny white balls. Perlite improves drainage and keeps the soil light and airy, giving plant roots enough oxygen.

VERMICULITE

Vermiculite is a natural mineral that expands when heated and looks like shiny, flaky particles. It holds water and nutrients, releasing them slowly to plants, and is great for keeping the soil moist. It's different from perlite in that it holds more water, while perlite focuses on drainage.

Adding a handful of compost keeps the plant productive.

WATER

Leonardo da Vinci knew what he was talking about when he declared, "Water is the driving force of all nature." You will soon discover that nothing in your garden will grow without water. That part might be obvious, but what's less obvious is that *how* you water your plants is every bit as important as ensuring you give them water at all.

This principle was certainly not obvious to us at first! When Marv got his first ever plant, the next thing we did was water the beautiful creature. He watered it daily, figuring that was part of "Being a Responsible Plant Owner 101." Wrong! Daily watering was far too often and actually just as harmful to the plant as if it were denied water entirely. The plant was overwatered and died quickly, an unfortunate casualty of Marv's education.

When it comes to watering plants, a good balance is required. Instead of watering lightly every day, aim for deep soaking sessions about 2 to 3 times per week. This encourages roots to grow deeper into the soil, promoting healthier plants.

DRIP IRRIGATION SYSTEMS IN A SMALL SPACE

Sometimes, when people on social media see pictures and videos of our backyard, they marvel at its size—how can one couple have all that greenery in the suburbs?! And they are correct to feel awe; we certainly do. But with more size comes more work and challenges. Lots more. When our garden grew bigger, with more areas to water, we started spending hours just watering our plants. We had to water before we went to work, and we never had time to do other things in the garden. It became overwhelming and untenable. If we had to water by hand everything we have in our backyard now, it would take us half a day. Plants are healthier on a consistent watering schedule.

We decided to add a drip irrigation system to our garden, which would eliminate the need to worry about constantly watering. We had never done a system like this before, and it felt a little intimidating. But after researching and watching YouTube videos, it was easier than we anticipated.

First, we measured our area and purchased the equipment we needed. It took a while to initially set up, but the amount of time we saved watering the garden by hand was enormous. We also noticed that the plants did much better with drip irrigation, since the water was slowly going deep into the roots. At the same time, we also reduced our water usage. Now, everything from pots on the ground to garden beds to grow bags and even the hanging baskets are on the same drip irrigation system. We also purchased a timer so that the garden is watered automatically every other day for 20 minutes in the morning.

Drip irrigation isn't necessary but it's useful, especially if you have a full-time job outside the home and want to consistently water your garden without it consuming all your time. We started with ½-inch tubing for distribution, which we then connected to ¼-inch drip irrigation tubing. We used two different connections: one using drip-emitter tubing with 12 inches of spacing, which is much easier to install and is ideal for garden beds or any containers that are next to each other, and a second connection, which is helpful for a longer line of grow bags. The second option is a standard ¼-inch tube without any holes, and we connected this using barbed tees and an emitter at the end to release the water. This option is helpful for containers, trees and shrubs, and especially vertical structures. With the second option, you have more control over water flow. Once it was all set up, we installed the water timer on our faucet and set it to release liquid every 2 days. If it rains, we extend the duration to every 3 days.

Inexpensive DIY irrigation, an effective way to water deeply while reducing surface evaporation.

USING BOTTLES TO WATER YOUR PLANTS

Reusing bottles to water your plants is an easy, eco-friendly, and effective way to keep them hydrated, especially if you're busy or away for a few days. Here are some simple methods to try.

HIDDEN-BOTTLE WATERING SYSTEMS

Take a plastic bottle (any regular soda or water bottle will do), and using a nail or pin, poke small holes in the sides or the bottom. The number and size of the holes will determine how quickly the water is released. Bury the bottle face up near the plant roots, exposing the top for easy refilling. Fill the bottle with water, and it will slowly release moisture into the soil over time. **Tip:** If you want to avoid plastic, use clay pots and seal the drainage hole with cork or fabric. Water will slowly soak through the porous clay walls, delivering moisture to the plant roots over time.

WINE-BOTTLE WATERING SYSTEM

Fill a glass wine bottle with water and insert it upside down into the soil near the plant roots. The soil will create a plug, which allows the water to seep out gradually as the soil dries. With this method your plant will remain hydrated for up to 3 days.

DIY DRIP IRRIGATION WITH PLASTIC BOTTLES

To water small pots easily, start by taking a plastic bottle and cutting off the bottom so you can refill it easily. Next, poke a small hole in the cap. Turn the bottle upside down and use string or tape to attach the body of the bottle to a stick. Then, push the stick into the soil on the inside wall of the pot so the bottle is hovering a little above the soil. This setup will let water drip out slowly, keeping your plants watered consistently.

WICKING WATERING SYSTEM

Gather a wick (cotton rope or fabric) and a water container like a bowl. Cut the wick long enough for it to reach from the bottom of the container to deep in the soil in your plant pot. Place one end in the water container and insert the other deep into the soil. Fill the container with water, ensuring the wick stays submerged. The wick will gradually draw water into the soil, keeping your plant hydrated. Check the soil regularly and monitor the water level, refilling the container as needed.

Capturing Rainwater

Rainwater is like magical water. Everything grows so much bigger and fuller with rainwater because it contains natural nutrients beneficial for plant growth. It has higher nitrogen levels, which is vital for plant health and promotes lush, green foliage. It is also rich in oxygen, which helps plants grow more vigorously. If you want to save yourself the effort, consider purchasing a rain barrel—it does much of the work for you. Char had been dreaming of having a rain barrel for years, but Marv only installed it for her in 2023. Char found a great deal on a barrel at the end of the season, which is the best time to find terrific sales on most garden equipment. We kept the barrels safe during the winter and by the spring, we were ready to install them. We placed them near a downspout and added a diverter to transfer water from the spout into the barrels. This year, we improved the rain barrels by adding a pump and a hose to make watering more convenient. Now we wish we had installed the barrels sooner!

SELF-WATERING CONTAINERS

A self-watering container is a special type of plant pot that has a built-in water reservoir at the bottom. This reservoir holds extra water, and the plant's roots (or a "wick," a material that absorbs water) slowly pulls the water up into the soil as needed.

WHY USE SELF-WATERING CONTAINERS?

- **Saves time:** You don't need to water your plants daily. Just refill the reservoir when it's low.
- **Prevents overwatering:** The plant only takes the water it needs, reducing the risk of root rot.
- **Conserves water:** Less water is wasted because it's stored in the reservoir and used gradually.
- **Great for busy people:** Perfect for those who forget to water their plants or are away for a few days.
- **Versatility:** Ideal for beginners, busy gardeners, or anyone growing plants in hot or dry climates where soil dries quickly.

Here are the steps for busy gardeners who want to devise a self-watering system that keeps plants hydrated for an extended period:

1. Get a standard-size container (we used the 17-gallon ones). In one of its sides, drill a small hole 2 to 3 inches from the bottom. This is where the water will drain out from the container.
2. Cut one end of a PVC pipe at an angle. The PVC pipe should be 3 to 4 inches taller than the container.
3. Cover corrugated drainpipes with weed barrier fabric and put them in the bottom of the container lengthwise. This will be the water reservoir in the base of your container. Make sure to cover both ends of the pipes with fabric to prevent soil from going in—this will act as the wick.
4. Insert the PVC pipe inside of the container with the angled side facing down, making sure it's placed next to the openings of the drainpipes.
5. Add soil and your plant(s).
6. For quick refills, you can water by inserting a hose into the PVC pipe. When the reservoir is full, water will flow out through the drain hole. Watering through the topsoil also works.

SEASONAL GARDENING
IN LIMITED SPACES

For those who live in colder climates, the growing season never seems long enough. But the good news is that utilizing season-extension techniques, like cold frames, row covers, hoop houses, or greenhouses, you can create a microclimate around your plants to extend your growing season. These structures protect plants from frost and cold temperatures, allowing you to harvest well into the fall and winter.

We mainly use our greenhouse to extend our season from spring all the way to the beginning of winter. By winter, we use the space to store our perennial plants in containers, giving them a better chance to survive and revive by the spring.

When using season extenders, make sure to select the correct vegetable varieties that don't mind a little cold weather. Crops that can tolerate coldness are carrots, rutabaga, turnips, cauliflower, kale, and brussels sprouts. Some veggies, like spinach, radishes, lettuce, and peas, even thrive in cooler temperatures. Also, consider fast-growing varieties that can be planted multiple times throughout the year to ensure a continuous supply of fresh produce.

We start planting outdoors in early April, as soon as the ground can be worked on or when the soil temperature is 45°F (7°C) or higher. Row covers—polyethylene plastic or fabrics that cover your planting area—can help keep the soil warm and protect your seedlings during those early, fragile weeks. Note that some plants grow better when they are planted directly in the ground. These include radishes, spinach, lettuce, turnips, arugula, carrots, and peas.

COLD FRAMES

A cold frame is like a mini greenhouse. It's basically a box without a bottom with a clear top that catches sunlight. The sun warms it up during the day, and at night it keeps your plants cozy. You can make one from old wood and a window, or buy one that's already made. Put it somewhere sunny facing south. They work great for growing lettuce and spinach all winter long.

ROW COVERS

These are like lightweight blankets you put over your plants when it gets frosty. They protect plants from the cold while still letting in light and water. They're perfect for protecting young plants in spring or for extending your harvest to go longer into the fall.

HOOP HOUSES

Make these by bending metal pipes into half-circles over your garden bed and covering them with plastic. They work like a greenhouse and can give you 4 to 6 extra weeks of growing time. Just remember to open them up on warm days or your plants will get too hot.

GREENHOUSES

Even a small greenhouse lets you grow warm-weather plants all year. They're cheaper and easier to set up than ever before. Add a small heater for really cold nights and you'll be amazed at what you can grow.

Build Your Own All-Season Garden Bed

Don't let cold weather cut your growing season short! Our easy-to-follow plan shows you how to build a raised bed with a simple plastic cover that works like a mini greenhouse. It keeps your plants warm when temperatures drop and protects them from bugs and bad weather. You can extend your harvest for weeks—or even months—beyond the usual season! When summer arrives, simply swap the plastic for a screen cover so your plants can breathe while staying safe from pests.

Ready to build yours? Turn to page 149 for the complete step-by-step guide.

Greenhouse growing means early harvests,
weeks ahead of outdoor plantings.

SUCCESSION PLANTING

Succession planting means to keep on planting so that as one crop finishes, another is ready to take its place. This method maximizes the use of space in your garden and ensures a continual harvest throughout the growing season. For example, after harvesting early spring greens, you can immediately plant summer crops like beans or squash.

INTERPLANTING

Interplanting is a gardening technique that involves growing more than one type of crop in the same area. This method can enhance the use of space and resources in a garden, allowing for a more diverse and productive growing environment. By planting different crops together, gardeners can utilize their available space more efficiently. For example, shallow-rooted plants like onions can be grown alongside deeper-rooted ones. By combining different crops, gardeners can potentially increase their overall yield from a given area. This is particularly useful in small-space gardening.

UNDERSTANDING TEMPERATURES

In 2016, after settling into a new house, we built our little garden space with three garden beds. We were excited to grow many vegetables and waited until May 24 to start planting. In Toronto, May 24 is "the date"—an unwritten rule—when you can safely plant outdoors without worrying about frost returning for another five or six months. We bought seedlings from a local nursery and planted everything we needed for the entire season. We anticipated they would be all the vegetables we would harvest for the growing season.

This seemed like a great plan, but we weren't maximizing what we could potentially grow. We later learned that we could stretch the season by planting cold crops directly in the ground as early as April. Crops like radishes, spinach, carrots, lettuce, beets, peas, and bok choy are great options to start in the spring season. To make early growing even more effective, we started building covers for our beds using polyethylene plastic and created hoop tunnels to protect the seedlings from frost. Now, by the month of May, we can harvest these cold hardy crops and plant summer crops like tomatoes, peppers, eggplants, zucchini, and more. When one crop finishes, we have seedlings or seeds ready to take that space, creating an endless harvest. By the end of summer (around August for us), we learned to start planting cold crops again, which benefit from the drop in temperature. Then, before winter arrives, we retrieve our covers to protect the plants from the cold weather. All of this extends our season all the way to the end of December, giving us an extra month or two of growth.

Keeping spring plantings warm through cold snaps and safe from pests.

Spring row covers take minutes to install and provide weeks of protection for young plants.

INDOOR GARDENING

The coldest the temperature in Ontario gets is usually around -22°F (-30°C). In certain regions in Canada, temps have dropped to as low as -40°F (-40°C)! But our winters are still cold enough to make it unbearable for certain plants to survive. We place polyethylene plastic covers over our garden to protect our plants from cold winds and frost. But while some plants can survive, there's no work we can do in the garden during winter. We don't water anything, and we rarely go out into our backyard this time of the year. We've tried to grow outdoors in midwinter, but the difficulty doesn't pay off. We prefer to grow our food indoors in the comfort of our home, where things can actually grow.

Indeed, indoor gardening can be an excellent way to grow food year-round, especially during colder months when outdoor gardening may not be feasible. Use windowsills or grow lights to cultivate herbs, microgreens, dwarf tomatoes, or dwarf peppers—experiment with what works for you. This approach allows you to maintain a steady supply of fresh produce regardless of the weather conditions.

Another way to extend your season is to start planting seeds early indoors and then transplant them in the garden once the risk of frost has passed. We like to start with tomatoes, peppers, and eggplants.

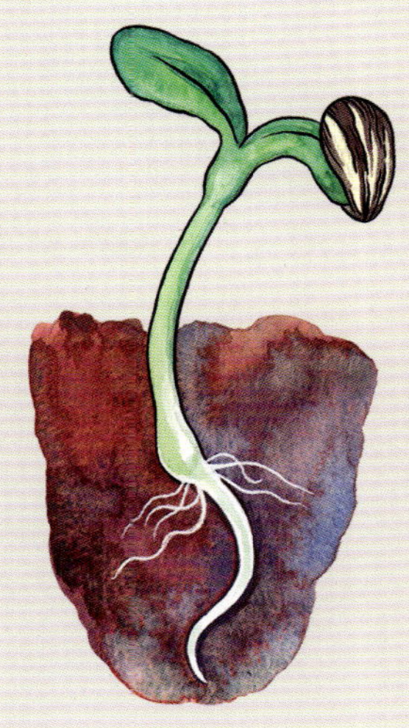

SEEDS AND SEEDLINGS

Every American knows the famous legend of Johnny Appleseed, the pioneer who introduced apple seed–growing to the midwestern United States. But he also was active in Ontario, so we Canadians share an affection for him as well. The guy knew his stuff: Growing vegetables from seeds is more cost-effective than purchasing seedlings from a nursery. When you grow vegetables from their seeds, you have access to a much broader selection of plant varieties than what is typically available at local nurseries. This diversity allows you to experiment with different flavors and colors, enhancing your gardening experience. Plus, starting your plants from seeds is an enjoyable activity to help you get through the winter season. On the flip side, purchasing grown seedlings also has benefits: It offers reliable choices, saves time, and is convenient. We like starting from seeds to get rare plants growing in our garden, but for you—don't be ashamed about opting for nursery-bought seedlings!

SEED BASICS

Here are some tips to start seeding and becoming a Johnny Appleseed yourself.

CHOOSING SEEDS

The right seeds are crucial for successful germination and growth. Consider factors such as your local climate, the growing season, and the specific varieties you wish to cultivate.

TIMING

Understanding when to start planting your seeds indoors is essential. A planting calendar is a valuable tool that has helped us get better at seed starting by enabling us to determine the best times to plant different types of vegetables, fruits, herbs, and flowers based on our location. (See planting calendars starting on page 229.) It lets us know when to sow seeds indoors or outdoors, transplant seedlings, and harvest crops. It also indicates the dates of our last spring frost and first fall frost as a reference point for determining planting times. Some calendars show whether a vegetable can be sown directly in the ground or if they fare better as seedlings starting indoors.

Seed starting success comes from knowing the basics—temperature preferences, moisture needs, and how deep to plant each variety.

SEED-STARTING SOIL MIX

A sterile seed-starting mix is essential for preventing diseases that can harm seedlings. A soil-less mix, often made from peat moss or coir, provides a clean environment for seeds to germinate without the pathogens present in garden soil. Seed-starting soil must be light and loose, making it easier for seeds to push through and sprout. It's widely available, but you can also use any homemade combination of coir, peat, perlite, worm castings, and compost. Make sure to remove any hard, solid pieces, like wood chips. Also, presoaking your soil blend with water will reduce seed disturbance.

When we started gardening, we didn't know what soil mix to use to pot seedlings. We tested many types of soil mixes and eventually landed on a good one, simple as it is: two parts coco coir and one part worm castings collected from vermicompost (alternatively, use finished compost from your garden as a substitute for worm castings).

This shows the value of composting food scraps and turning it into black gold. Some of the plants grew bigger, but what we liked about this mix the most was its consistency when it came to growing different varieties. When you pot up again, the plants will be bigger and require additional nutrients, so double up on worm castings or compost, or add other fertilizers, like diluted fish emulsion.

We've found our perfect germination mix—just
coco coir and worm castings, simple but effective.

SOAKING SEEDS

Although it's not entirely necessary to soak your seeds, it helps break down the seed's exterior coating, promoting a more successful germination. We like to soak legume, corn, pepper, eggplant, and tomato seeds in warm water. The duration of soaking varies:

- **Beans (e.g., kidney, pinto):** Soak for 8 to 12 hours. Beans have hard seed coats that benefit from soaking.
- **Peas (e.g., garden peas):** Soak for 8 to 12 hours.
- **Corn:** Soak for 12 to 24 hours. Corn seeds are relatively large and can absorb moisture quickly.
- **Squash (e.g., zucchini, pumpkin):** Soak for 6 to 8 hours. Squash seeds can benefit from soaking but do not need to be soaked for as long as beans or corn do.
- **Cucumbers:** Soak for 6 to 8 hours.
- **Tomatoes:** Soak for 2 to 4 hours. While not necessary, soaking can help if the seeds are particularly dry.
- **Peppers:** Soak for 8 to 12 hours. Soaking helps soften the hard seed coat.

DEPTH

Some seeds require exposure to light to start the germination process, while others rely on darkness. Here is a simple rule for optimal seed germination and growth: Plant seeds at a depth that is twice their diameter. This principle is based on the idea that seeds need adequate soil coverage to retain moisture and to protect them from environmental factors while ensuring they are not buried too deeply, which could hinder their ability to sprout. For example, if a seed has a diameter of half an inch (1.27cm), it should be planted at a depth of 1 inch (2.54cm).

The minimum depth for tiny seeds like lettuce or basil is typically around ¼ inch. These tiny seeds are sensitive to light and moisture and can therefore be pressed into the soil surface with just a sprinkle of soil on top. Medium-size seeds, like tomatoes or brassicas, should generally be sown at a depth equal to about twice their diameter. For example, a tomato seed about ⅛ inch in diameter should be planted approximately ¼ inch deep. Larger seeds, such as beans or squash, can be planted deeper—typically at a depth of 1 to 2 inches. These seeds require more soil coverage to retain moisture and protect them from pests.

Measure the right depth before planting the seed in the soil.

SCARIFICATION

Scarification involves nicking or sanding the seed coat to help the seeds absorb water more effectively, thereby promoting quicker and more reliable germination. Okra, nasturtium, pumpkin, peppers, bitter melon, and New Zealand spinach all benefit from this process.

How to Nick Seeds

STEP 1: Use a sharp tool, such as a knife or nail clipper to make a shallow cut on the seed coat without damaging the inner embryo.

STEP 2: Soak the seeds in water for several hours or overnight, before planting directly into soil.

SEED-STARTING EQUIPMENT

CONTAINERS

Seeds can be started in various containers, pots, or repurposed items, like takeout containers. Ensure that whatever container you use has drainage holes to prevent waterlogging.

Depending on your seeds, you may opt for differently sized containers. For example, we use smaller sizes for peppers and tomatoes and then up the pot to a bigger container when they have grown a bit, since they sprout and grow much slower than other veggies. For squash, use bigger containers from the outset, since they are fast sprouting and require much more room to grow.

SOIL BLOCK

If you choose not to use plastic containers, you can go with a soil-blocking method—freestanding cubes of compressed soil made using a tool called a soil blocker. The blocks are created from a specialized soil mix that is moist enough to hold its shape.

SEED TRAY

Some trays have up to seventy-six cells per tray, which will allow you to grow multiple seedlings in a single tray. This works best for fast-growing crops like lettuce, spinach, and onions that can be planted immediately without needing to up pot.

BOTTOM TRAYS

No matter what type of seed-starting containers you choose, you'll need sturdy bottom trays to catch water and make moving seedlings easier. We've been using high-quality 10x20-inch trays for a while now, which are very durable.

Soil blocks save space and materials: no pots to wash, no plastic waste, just perfectly formed seedling cubes ready to plant.

HUMIDITY DOME

Covering your seed tray with a dome increases humidity, creating an optimal environment for seeds to sprout. We've sprouted both with and without a cover, and the covered seeds always have the best germination rate. As soon as the seeds sprout, the covers should be removed.

LABELS

Labeling your seedlings is essential for keeping track of different plant varieties. It's a simple step that prevents confusion as your seedlings grow and start to look similar. Early on in our gardening journey, we used permanent markers to label our plants, but over time, the writing would smudge or fade from watering, leaving us with mystery plants!

Now, we've upgraded to a waterproof label printer, allowing us to create labels that stick onto popsicle sticks. These labels stand up to moisture and can be reused year after year, making them a durable and sustainable option. Of course, there are plenty of ways to label your plants, such as plastic plant tags, which are durable and reusable and can be written on with permanent markers; wooden popsicle sticks, which are inexpensive, biodegradable, and easy to write on; and tape labels, which can be as easy as attaching painter's tape or masking tape to containers and writing on them with permanent marker.

WATERING

Proper watering techniques are vital for seed germination. Overwatering can lead to damping off, a fungal disease. Bottom watering is often recommended, as it allows moisture to wick up through the soil without dislodging delicate seeds.

Bottom watering lets seedlings drink from below—roots grow downward, seeking moisture, while soil surface stays dry.

Grow lights stop seedlings from stretching, producing vigorous, stocky starts.

LIGHT

Once seedlings emerge, they require adequate light to grow strong and healthy. Natural sunlight from windows is often insufficient for indoor seed starting, but using grow lights can help ensure seedlings receive the consistent, bright light they need to prevent leggy growth and develop properly.

There's no need to keep your seed tray under the light before they sprout. At the outset, placing your tray in a warm location is more important. When they do sprout, however, it's time to expose the seedlings to the light. Grow lights help prevent lanky growth and are a good investment if you plan on seeding a lot and yearly. Lanky growth occurs when seedlings don't get enough light, causing them to stretch upward and develop tall and weak stems instead of strong and sturdy ones. Ensure your seedlings receive adequate light, ideally 12 to 16 hours daily. Place your grow light about 8 inches above seedlings and adjust accordingly as the plant grows. If you opt for natural light, place the tray near a bright window where the seedlings can get at least 6 hours of sun exposure. Rotate the tray every day for even exposure.

TEMPERATURE

Maintaining an appropriate temperature is critical for seed germination. Most seeds (like most people) prefer a warm environment (around 70°F or 21°C). Heat mats can be used to maintain a stable temperature. For most seeds, a stable temperature between 70°F and 85°F (21°C to 29°C) is ideal for optimal growth. Cold crops can germinate at a slightly lower temperature, around 50°F to 65°F (10°C to 18°C).

AIR CIRCULATION

Good air circulation helps prevent diseases like damping off. You can use a small fan on a low setting to promote airflow around your seedlings. Having a small fan will also help to strengthen your seedlings. If you prefer to strengthen seedlings manually, gently brush your hands through the seedlings from time to time.

Running a fan over seedlings mimics outdoor breezes, creating stronger, more resilient plants.

FERTILIZING

Worm castings are an excellent organic fertilizer rich in nutrients and beneficial microorganisms. When your seedlings have developed their first true leaves, you can start fertilizing them with worm castings. Mix the worm castings into the soil at a ratio of about 10 percent worm castings to 90 percent potting mix, or sprinkle a thin layer on top of the soil and gently work it in. Fertilize every 2 to 4 weeks, depending on your plant's growth stage and specific needs.

Fish emulsion is another excellent choice for seedlings because it provides a gentle, nutrient-rich boost that supports early growth stages without overwhelming them. Fish emulsion contains essential nutrients, like nitrogen, which helps seedlings grow lush green leaves, and phosphorus, which supports strong root development and is crucial for young plants. It also provides potassium, which makes seedlings more resilient.

UP POTTING

When seeding plants indoors, plan to have room for up potting. Keep an eye on roots exiting the bottom of the seed tray, as it's a sign to move the plants to a bigger container. It is essential to up pot your seedlings, as they can get rootbound, which means their roots have outgrown the container they are in and have started circling around the edges of the pot instead of spreading out. This can have several adverse effects on the plant's growth and health.

When up potting a seedling or plant, the general rule of thumb is to choose a pot that is 1 to 2 inches larger in diameter than the current pot. This gradual increase in size allows the plant's roots to expand into the new soil without overwhelming them with too much space.

From seed to transplant, we produce
hundreds of healthy plants indoors.

HARDENING OFF SEEDLINGS

Plant hardening, or "hardening off," is like training your plants to survive the outdoors. Imagine you stayed inside all winter and then suddenly spent a whole day outside in the blazing sun—you'd probably get sunburned or feel overwhelmed! Plants are the same. If they've grown indoors, they need time to adjust to the harsher outdoor environment before being planted in the garden.

THINGS TO KEEP IN MIND BEFORE STARTING

- **Timing:** Begin the hardening-off process about 1 to 2 weeks before you plan to transplant your seedlings outdoors. This allows enough time for them to adjust gradually.
- **Choose a stable outdoor spot:** Select a location where your plants can remain throughout the hardening-off process. If possible, this spot should initially be shaded and protected from strong winds.

STEPS TO HARDENING OFF SEEDLINGS

1. For days 1 and 2, cover your plants with a tarp or shade cloth to shield them from direct sunlight. The cover acts as a buffer, reducing the intensity of sunlight and protecting plants from sudden exposure to outdoor conditions.

2. On days 3 and 4, gradually remove the tarp or shade cloth during sunny periods in the morning or late afternoon each day. Monitor weather conditions: If there's an unexpected frost warning or extreme weather, bring the plants indoors.

3. By days 5 to 7, your plants should be ready to handle full sun exposure. Be sure to water well during this process; open air also helps the seedlings adjust much faster.

4. After the hardening-off process, the seedlings can be transplanted to their final spot. Make sure to plant them in the evening or on a cloudy day to reduce stress.

Hardening off prepares indoor seedlings for outdoor life.

TRANSPLANTING YOUR SEEDLINGS

Transplanting is an essential step to ensuring your seedlings thrive in your garden. Before transplanting, prepare your garden bed by loosening the soil and adding compost or well-rotted manure to improve fertility and drainage. Transplant seedlings outdoors after the last frost date in your area and when they have developed at least two sets of true leaves, indicating they are strong enough to handle outdoor conditions.

TRANSPLANTING PROCESS

Water your seedlings thoroughly before transplanting to reduce stress. Dig holes in your garden bed that are slightly larger than the root ball of each seedling. Carefully remove each seedling from its container, taking care not to damage the roots. Place each seedling into its hole at the same depth at which it was growing in its container. Then, fill around it with soil, and gently pat down. Water immediately after transplanting to help settle the soil around the roots. After transplanting, continue to monitor your plants closely for signs of stress and provide adequate water and care as they settle into their new environment.

TIPS

Handle with care: Hold small seedlings by their leaves instead of the stem. A damaged leaf can regrow, but a crushed stem won't survive.

Wilting after transplant? This is normal for the first day or two. Provide shade if wilting persists beyond 48 hours.

Leggy seedlings? Plant them deeper than normal (except for tomatoes, which benefit from deep planting regardless).

Water wisely: Keep soil consistently moist but not waterlogged for the first week.

Evening or cloudy day transplanting reduces stress on seedlings.

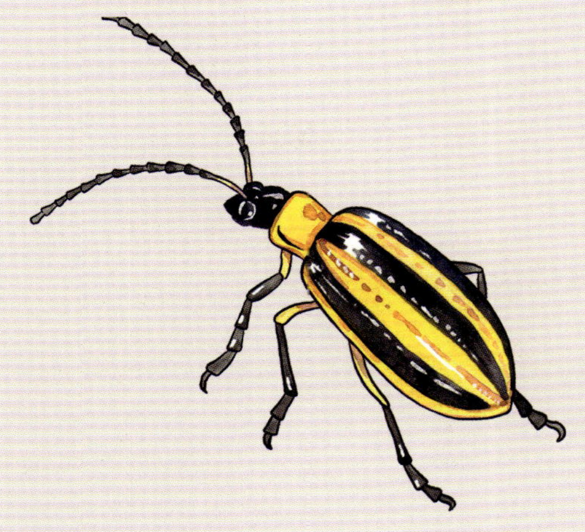

PEST AND DISEASE MANAGEMENT

If you cultivate a garden—any garden, anywhere—you *will* encounter pests and unwanted creatures that find the plants and vegetables you're growing delicious, hospitable, or both. Bugs and gardening go together like love and marriage, a horse and carriage, and whatever else the song says. If you work outside, dealing with these creatures is sadly unavoidable. Unfortunately, some would-be gardeners let the prospect of insects and other associated critters deter them from getting their hands dirty in the soil. But with the proper strategies, you can prevent pests from destroying your hard work.

NATURAL PEST CONTROL METHODS

The best, most organic way to take care of unwanted pests is by building a great garden ecosystem and letting nature do the work. Nature has evolved in such a way that its elements balance each other out, creating something approaching harmony. For instance, while ladybugs might look unsightly, they can become your garden's protectors; these red-and-black insects enjoy feasting on pesky pests without harming your plants.

Similarly, planting flowers will have a huge impact on your vegetable garden. Not only do flowers enhance the visual appeal of your garden space, but they also contribute to a healthier, more productive garden ecosystem by attracting beneficial insects, aiding in natural pest control, and promoting pollination for a more rewarding harvest. Initially, we planted only vegetables in our garden, but after introducing flowers, we spent less time dealing with pests, our garden was full of life, and our harvest improved! The difference was significant.

This process is called "companion planting," where certain plants are introduced to repel or deter pests, keeping your garden harmonious and pest-free. For instance, the scent of marigolds can deter rabbits from feasting on your leafy greens, and you can plant them as borders around your garden bed to act like a natural barrier. Vegetables and roses also mix well in the garden. Since our roses started blooming, we've noticed that Japanese beetles enjoy hanging out on the roses instead of the vegetable plants. The roses are essentially the perfect trap, giving us time to remove the insects before they cause too much damage to the flowers, and especially to the vegetables that we really prize.

Sometimes, despite these techniques, you need to step in and lend a hand to balance things out. If all else fails, the best tried-and-true method for us is to remove unwanted bugs by hand. Gypsy moth caterpillars can decimate an entire tree or shrub if left unchecked; they like to go after our red currant bush plant each year, so we reluctantly step in and remove them by hand. Wasps hunt the remaining caterpillars. Similarly, slugs are relentless, like zombies in a horror movie or telemarketers who know you can't resist answering the phone. Handpicking can be an effective method to control the slug population, lest they terrorize your backyard utopia. This is best done during rainy weather when slugs are most active, as the increased moisture levels create favorable breeding grounds. You can also attack these creatures at night or in the early morning, when the soil is moist. Currently, we're winning the battle against these insects by combining handpicking with copper mesh, which can be wrapped around a pot, the base of a plant, or the entire edge of a garden bed to prevent slugs from crossing over or climbing on to the plant leaves and fruits. But truth be told, the war never ends.

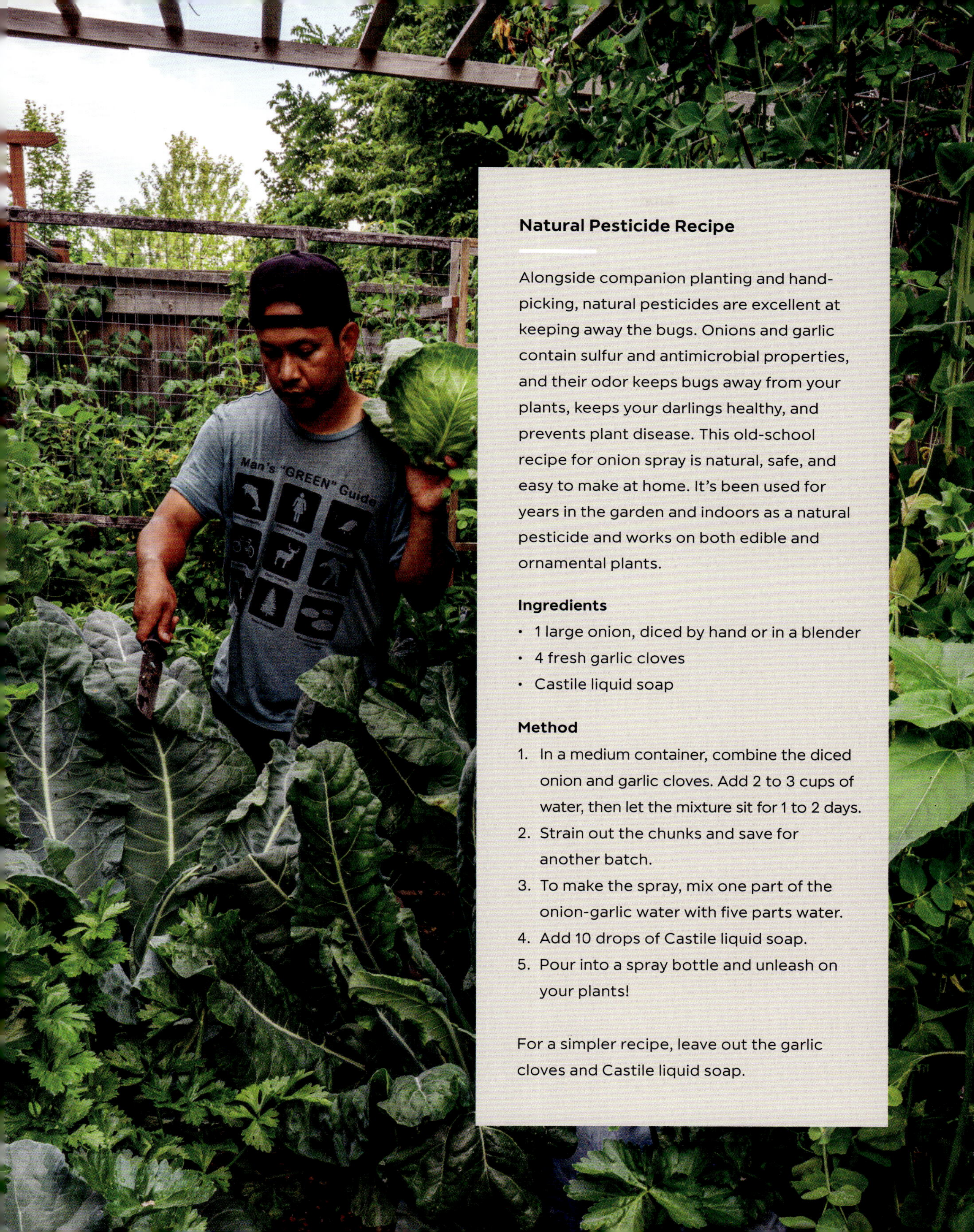

Natural Pesticide Recipe

Alongside companion planting and hand-picking, natural pesticides are excellent at keeping away the bugs. Onions and garlic contain sulfur and antimicrobial properties, and their odor keeps bugs away from your plants, keeps your darlings healthy, and prevents plant disease. This old-school recipe for onion spray is natural, safe, and easy to make at home. It's been used for years in the garden and indoors as a natural pesticide and works on both edible and ornamental plants.

Ingredients
- 1 large onion, diced by hand or in a blender
- 4 fresh garlic cloves
- Castile liquid soap

Method
1. In a medium container, combine the diced onion and garlic cloves. Add 2 to 3 cups of water, then let the mixture sit for 1 to 2 days.
2. Strain out the chunks and save for another batch.
3. To make the spray, mix one part of the onion-garlic water with five parts water.
4. Add 10 drops of Castile liquid soap.
5. Pour into a spray bottle and unleash on your plants!

For a simpler recipe, leave out the garlic cloves and Castile liquid soap.

Ladybugs provide natural pest control.

We plant flowers throughout the garden to attract essential pollinators.

Diverse plants attract beneficial insects in the garden.

CREATING BIODIVERSITY IN SMALL AREAS

Along with protecting your beautiful space from unwanted intruders, creating and preserving biodiversity in your garden is a great way to care for our environment. Even with a small backyard garden, regenerative agriculture practices can still be applied. The goal is to build a healthy ecosystem and let nature do its work in a cohesive environment. You can enhance biodiversity with diverse plantings that attract various beneficial insects to create a balanced ecosystem. Remember: A thriving garden is a sustainable garden, where nature's solutions reign supreme!

Here are a few practices you can apply in your garden to improve the health of your soil, build a garden ecosystem, and help the environment:

1. Avoid tilling your soil. No-till gardening protects beneficial soil organisms like earthworms and microbes while preserving surface habitat for advantageous insects and wildlife.
2. Plant a wide variety of plants that attract different types of insects and birds.
3. Apply a crop rotation technique, which prevents pest and disease buildup and supports different beneficial insects and soil microbes with varied climate preferences.
4. Plant perennials. Perennial fruits are the ultimate garden treasures. With endless harvests year after year, these plants are a fruit lover's dream come true. We enjoy apples, strawberries, black currants, red currants, and plums. Note that blackberries should be grown near a trellis because they can vine and spread fast, like a good rumor.
5. Engage with your community, connect with neighbors, and share your knowledge and resources.
6. Conserve water in your garden by adding water sources such as birdbaths, ponds, or streams.
7. Include features that provide nesting sites and shelter for wildlife.

Copper mesh around the stem helps keep slugs away. Contact with the copper creates a mild reaction that slugs find unpleasant.

PESTS: A GARDENER'S GUIDE

ANTS

You're probably familiar with ants—those tiny bugs that like to walk in straight lines. You often see them near plants such as citrus trees, which also attract aphids. To eliminate ants naturally, sprinkle diatomaceous earth around their trails or on the affected plants, and keep your garden clean by removing food scraps. You can also spray citrus oil on the soil or directly on the ants.

APHIDS

Aphids are small, soft bugs that can be green, black, or brown, and they usually hang out on the undersides of leaves, sucking out the plant's juices and causing leaves to curl or turn yellow. You can wash them off with a strong spray of water mixed with a natural insecticidal soap, or bring in ladybugs and lacewings, which love to eat aphids.

EARWIGS

Earwigs are dark brown bugs with pincers that enjoy hiding in damp areas like mulch or dead leaves. To remove them naturally, roll up wet newspapers and leave them in the affected areas. The earwigs will use the papers as a hiding spot. Carefully remove the papers in the morning. You can also use small containers filled with oil and soy sauce to trap them.

FRUIT FLIES

Fruit flies are tiny tan or brown flies that buzz around overripe fruits or compost. To deal with these pests, pour apple cider vinegar into a bowl, cover it with plastic wrap, and poke small holes into the film to trap them.

PILL BUGS

Pill bugs, also called roly-polies, are small gray insects that curl into balls when touched, and prefer damp areas. To manage them, reduce moisture in the garden and clean up hiding spots. You can also lay down damp toilet paper rolls for them to hide in, making it easier to remove them by hand, and sprinkle diatomaceous earth where you notice them.

LEAF MINERS

Leaf miners are small insect larvae that, as adults, look like black flies, often with a prominent yellow triangle between the bases of their wings. They live inside leaves and create squiggly trails as they eat. To stop them naturally, pick off the damaged leaves and throw them away, being sure to keep them away from the compost bin. Cover your plants with netting to prevent adult flies from laying eggs on the leaves.

CABBAGE MOTHS

Cabbage moths emerge from green caterpillars that chew big holes in the leaves of cabbage, broccoli, and kale plants. To control these pests naturally, cover your plants with floating row covers to stop the moths from laying eggs, and remove green caterpillars by hand. Adult cabbage moths resemble small white butterflies, and their eggs, which are very small, oval, and laid singly, can be spotted under the leaves.

SLUGS

Slugs are slimy creatures that leave a trail of their ooze behind them as they move. They create big holes in leaves as they eat, usually at night. To handle them, you can pick them off your plants in the evening or after a rainy day. Set out shallow dishes of beer (yes, beer!) to attract and drown them. For a nonlethal approach, you can wrap pots, plant stems, and garden beds with copper mesh.

SPIDER MITES

Spider mites are tiny pests almost like little spiders that turn leaves yellow or speckled, and their webs are often a giveaway of their presence. To get rid of them naturally, spray your plants with water to knock the mites off, use insecticidal soap, and keep your plants' leaves more humid, as spider mites love dry conditions.

SQUASH VINE BORERS

Adult squash vine borers have a distinctive appearance that resembles a wasp's, but the moth larvae burrow into squash stems, making them wilt and even die. To stop them naturally, cover the plants with row covers to block adult moths from laying eggs, which look like tiny bronze dots. Scrape off any eggs you see right away. You can also sprinkle diatomaceous earth around the base of the stems.

SQUIRRELS

Squirrels are furry little animals that love to munch on fruits, nuts, or vegetables in your garden. To keep them away naturally, use netting or hardware cloth to block access to plants, or scare them off with shiny objects like foil, reflective tape, or scarecrows. You can also provide a water bowl for wildlife since thirsty animals often bite into tomatoes just to get moisture.

BIRDS

Birds often peck at fruits, seeds, or vegetables in gardens and can cause a lot of damage. To protect your garden naturally, use bird netting to cover your plants, hang shiny reflective tape or fake predators like plastic owls to scare them off, or plant some decoy crops to distract them from your main plants.

CUCUMBER BEETLES

Cucumber beetles are small bugs that can be either striped or spotted and usually hang out on cucumber, squash, and melon plants. Look for these tiny beetles on the leaves or flowers of your plants; they cause damage by eating the leaves and laying eggs in the soil. You can physically pick them off the plants and drop them into a bucket of soapy water, as well as place thick straw or mulch around the base of your plants, which makes it harder for the beetles to lay their eggs. If you have a large infestation, consider applying a kaolin-clay-and-water spray to the leaves and stems.

JAPANESE BEETLES

Japanese beetles are shiny, metallic green bugs with coppery wings that love to munch on a wide variety of plants, including beans and grapes. To get rid of Japanese beetles, gently knock them off the plants into a bucket of soapy water, and use trap crops, like roses, to keep them off your fruits and vegetables.

Plant colorful flowers to draw Japanese beetles to them instead of your prized garden plants.

Not every leaf is perfect; some damage is part of growing organically and supporting biodiversity.

DISEASES

BLOSSOM-END ROT

Blossom-end rot looks like a dark, sunken spot at the bottom of fruits, including tomatoes, peppers, and squash. It starts small but gets bigger and eventually turns black or leathery. The disease occurs because the plant isn't getting enough calcium, often due to inconsistent watering. To combat blossom-end rot, water your plants regularly and add calcium to the soil using a calcium-rich fertilizer, such as gypsum.

BLIGHT

Blight causes brown or black spots on leaves, stems, or fruits, causing the plant to look wilted or simply die quickly. To fix blight, remove any infected leaves or plants and discard them. Water the base of the plant instead of the leaves, and use a natural fungicide like copper spray to protect healthy plants. You can also use a mix of oil, baking soda, and water as a spray to help contain blight.

LEAF CURL

Leaf curl makes leaves twist, curl up, or turn yellow or red. This can occur in fruit trees, tomatoes, or peppers and is typically caused by pests such as aphids or sometimes by environmental stress. For this disease, spray the affected plant with insecticidal soap to kill the pests, and make sure the plant gets enough water and nutrients, like from kelp meal.

MAGNESIUM DEFICIENCY

If a plant has a magnesium deficiency, the leaves will turn yellow between the veins while the veins themselves stay green. This usually appears first in older leaves. To address magnesium deficiency, water the plant with a ratio of one tablespoon Epsom salt mixed into 1 gallon of water.

NITROGEN DEFICIENCY

Nitrogen deficiency causes the leaves to turn light green or yellow, starting with the older leaves at the bottom. The affected plant may also grow slowly or look weak. To fix this, add compost, manure, or a nitrogen-rich fertilizer such as blood meal to the soil.

PHOSPHORUS DEFICIENCY

When a plant lacks phosphorus, its leaves may turn dark green or purple, and the plant may grow slowly or produce fewer flowers and fruits. For phosphorus-deficient plants, add bone meal, rock phosphate, or a phosphorus-rich fertilizer to the soil.

POTASSIUM DEFICIENCY

Potassium deficiency makes the edges of leaves turn yellow or brown, and the plant may look weak or produce small fruits. To combat this deficiency, add wood ash, compost, potash, or a potassium-rich fertilizer like kelp meal to the soil.

POWDERY MILDEW

A white, powdery coating resembling sprinkled flour on leaves, stems, or flowers is a telltale sign of a problem. Powdery mildew thrives in humid conditions. To get rid of powdery mildew, trim back crowded areas to improve airflow and spray the plant with a mixture of one quart water and one teaspoon baking soda.

ROOT ROT

Root rot causes plants to appear wilted, even when the soil is moist. The roots, when inspected, will look brown and mushy or have a bad smell. Root rot happens when the soil is too wet. For plants suffering from root rot, ensure the soil drains well and stop overwatering. If the plant is potted, repot it in fresh, dry soil and cut off any rotted roots.

RUST

Rust shows up as orange, yellow, or brown spots or bumps on leaves and commonly affects roses, beans, and hollyhocks. To address rust, remove the infected leaves and throw them away (don't compost them!). Spray the plant with a natural fungicide to prevent rust from spreading.

LEAF SPOTTING

Leaf spotting causes small, round spots on leaves that can be brown, black, or yellow. Over time, these spots may grow and lead to leaf drop. To fix leaf spotting, remove the infected leaves, and avoid watering the leaves directly. Use a natural fungicide, like copper spray, to protect healthy leaves.

INDOOR GARDENING

Canada is a wonderful country for many reasons, but its climate presents unique challenges for gardeners. It's not uncommon for much of our country to hover below 50°F (10°C) for six months of the year, and sometimes it gets far below zero, the type of cold where your nostrils sting just from breathing. Needless to say, it's enticing for most gardeners to close up shop for this period, deciding that braving the elements isn't worth the hassle. We can't blame them. But once we enjoyed cultivating our backyard paradise, we decided we couldn't give up the unmatched thrill of growing our own vegetables and plants. So we decided to bring our outdoor dreamscape indoors. With the techniques we cover in this chapter, we've been able to grow our food 365 days a year. Aside from enjoying the work itself, it's also rewarding to have access to our garden year-round and to rely less on buying greens from the store.

WHY GROW FOOD INDOORS?

True, growing food indoors means that you're, well, indoors, so you miss out on the beauty of being out in the world, under the sky, and directly in the earth. But gardening indoors gives you far more control over temperature, humidity, and light exposure than you could ever obtain in the great outdoors. You can also maximize your space by setting up vertical growing systems that can accommodate a variety of plants in a limited area. And, last but not least, there are no bugs inside, meaning lower risk of pests and diseases in general! That's no small advantage for those of us who hate insects.

We typically start setting up our indoor garden in late fall, close to the winter season. You might be in a similar situation where it's either too cold or too hot to garden outdoors, or you simply don't have the backyard space. If any of these cases apply, indoor gardening is a great option for you.

However, nature evolved to grant plants everything they need to survive—while your home didn't. It's essential to understand what your plants require to survive so you can provide them with the necessary environment and nutrients to grow healthy and strong.

LIGHTING

In indoor environments, natural light may not always be sufficient for optimal plant growth. This is especially true if you're growing in a basement or an apartment with limited exposure to the sun. And since many people who grow indoors are doing so because the outdoors is too cold, the season inherently has minimal hours of daylight. Grow lights can be used to supplement natural light or even replace it entirely, allowing plants to receive the energy they need regardless of the season or weather conditions. When you're growing indoors, consider using LED grow lights, which are more energy-efficient.

In general, you should provide your plants with at least 14 to 16 hours of light daily for optimal growth. If you prefer natural lighting, place your container near a window that receives at least 6 to 8 hours of sunlight. One of the best vegetable grow lights we've used is the SF600 from Spider Farmer. It only consumes a highly efficient 74 watts of power, which saves on energy costs over time, and provides full-spectrum, sunlike light with a 120-degree beam that ranges from red to blue to white, making it perfect for plant germination, flowering, and fruiting. Aside from being helpful for growing food year-round, these lights can also aid in starting your seedlings for the next growing season.

Supplemental grow lights make indoor gardening successful and productive.

Shelving units are ideal for small space growing—up instead of out.

THE KRATKY SYSTEM

The Kratky system is a passive hydroponic technique for growing plants suspended above the water level, into which their roots grow down to absorb the nutrients. As the plant consumes the water and nutrients, the water level gradually decreases, exposing more of its root system to the air, which helps provide oxygen to the roots to promote healthy growth. This is a low-maintenance and straightforward method that's ideal for small-scale indoor gardening. The Kratky system is a noncirculating technique, meaning no additional inputs of water or nutrients are needed after the original application, and no electricity, pumps, or water and oxygen circulation systems are required. All you have to do is establish a container with enough water and nutrients to last the plant's lifespan. Typically, you'll need an opaque tote bin of 2 gallons or more (to prevent algae), a net pot, and a growing medium such as clay pebbles or perlite. Choose a lid that is sturdy enough to cut without cracking, yet food-safe for edibles. Cut holes in the lid to match your net pot diameter—for example, a 2-inch pot requires a 2-inch hole.

Kratky hydroponics requires minimal equipment—set it up and let plants absorb nutrients as they grow.

SETTING UP AN INDOOR KRATKY GARDEN

Here is a step-by-step guide to building your paradise between four walls using the Kratky system:

PREPARE SEEDS

Begin by germinating your seeds. Fast-growing crops like lettuce, bok choy, arugula, radish, and spinach work best indoors. Place the seeds directly into your growing medium. If using Rockwool cubes, ensure they are presoaked and moist.

SET UP THE KRATKY SYSTEM

Fill whatever storage tote bin you have with water, and add the appropriate amount of nutrient solution according to the manufacturer's instructions. We use an organic liquid nutrient solution that we purchase locally, but many are available online. We also sometimes make our own nutrients using worm castings, Epsom salt, and kelp. A Kratky system doesn't require an air pump or refilling, as it's meant for vegetables that grow quickly and are harvested immediately.

PLANT SEEDS

Once your seeds have germinated and developed small roots (usually within 4 to 7 days), transplant them into your Kratky system's net pots filled with LECA clay pebbles. Make sure the roots are submerged in the nutrient solution while keeping the top of the plant above water.

HARVEST AND PLANT AGAIN

One week before you harvest, start planting more seeds for continuous growth. By harvest time, your seedlings should be ready to be transplanted.

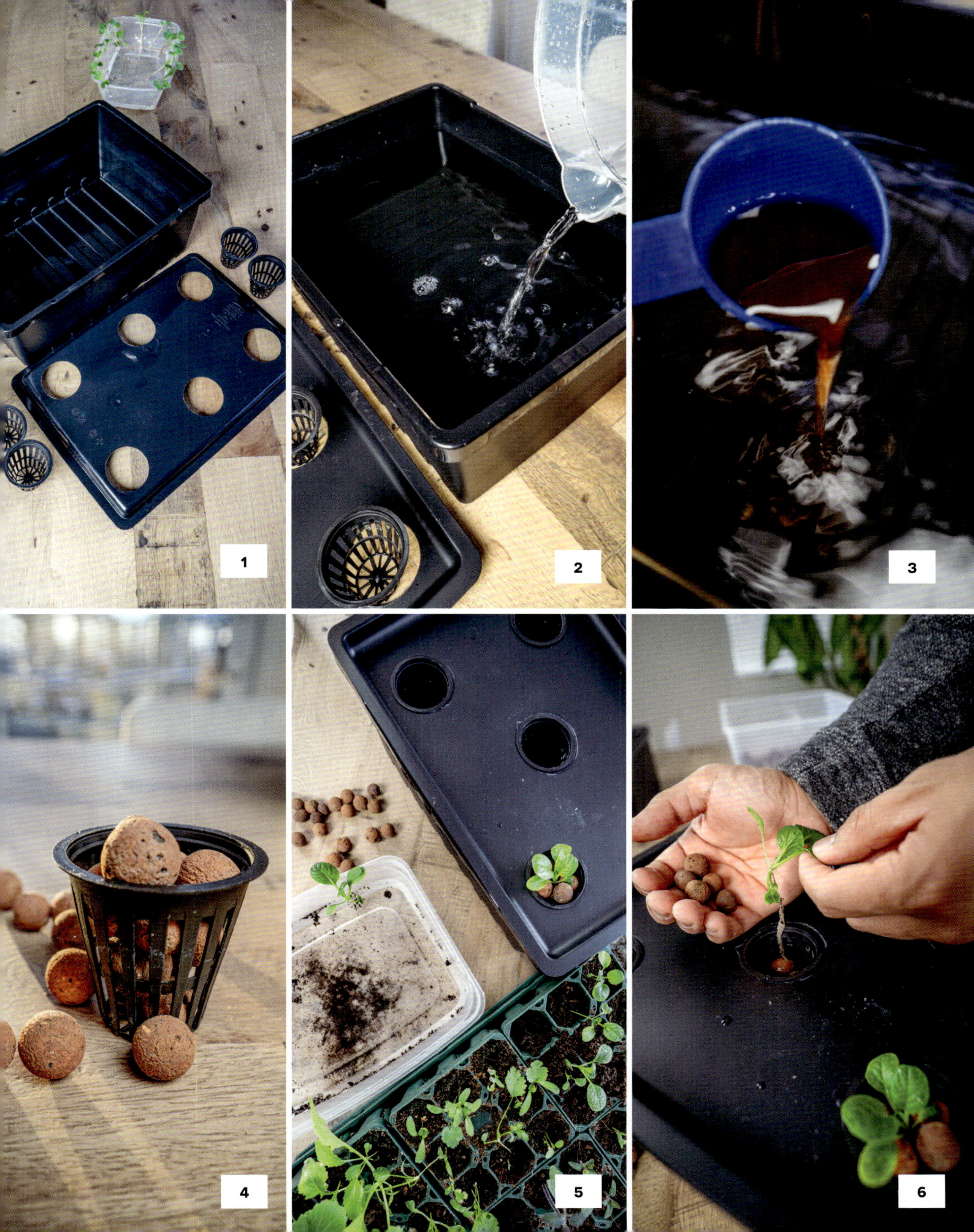

Easy Vegetables to Grow
in a Hydroponic System

• Arugula
• Basil
• Broccoli
• Cauliflower
• Chives
• Cilantro
• Cucumber
• Eggplant
• Green beans
• Kale
• Lettuce
• Parsley
• Pepper
• Spearmint
• Spinach
• Tomato

DEEP-WATER CULTURE

Deep-water culture (DWC) is a hydroponic growing method that involves suspending plant roots in a well-oxygenated nutrient solution 24/7. This system uses water efficiently and the constant oxygenation of the nutrient solution promotes healthy root development and nutrient absorption. It's similar to Kratky, with the only difference being that DWC uses an air pump and air stone to provide oxygen. This is ideal for plants that require extended growth periods, such as peppers and tomatoes.

Space-saving micro tomatoes are perfect for our indoor hydroponic system.

SETTING UP A DEEP-WATER CULTURE SYSTEM

Materials and Tools Needed

- 10-gallon container with lid to hold the water and nutrient solution
- Organic hydroponic liquid nutrient solution containing the necessary nutrients for plant growth
- Net pots to hold the plants and allow roots to grow into the nutrient solution below
- Air pump, air stone, and airline tubing that's 3/16" thick to oxygenate the nutrient solution
- Clay pebbles or another growing medium to support the plants and provide stability
- Hole saw

Steps

1. Drill a small hole on the top side of the container through which the airline tubing can pass.
2. Using a hole saw, cut a few holes in the container lid to match the net pots you will be using (e.g., for a 3-inch net pot, cut a 3-inch hole).
3. Connect one end of the airline tubing to the air pump (we use one with four outlets), pass it through the hole you drilled, and insert the other end into the air stone inside the container.
4. Fill the container with cold water. We put 8 gallons of water into our 10-gallon container to prevent overflow. As long as the bottom of the net pot is submerged in at least 1 inch of water, that is sufficient.
5. Add the appropriate amount of plant-based organic liquid nutrients according to the manufacturer's instructions.
6. To start the seedlings, we recommend planting them with coco coir under a grow light. This enables you to remove the coco coir and rinse the root in water before transferring them to the hydroponic system.
7. To keep the seedlings above the water level, use LECA clay pebbles, which are reusable and provide excellent drainage, aeration, and root support for hydroponic systems.
8. To save on energy, consider running your system at night, during off-peak hours, which is what we do!

DIY PROJECTS FOR COMPACT GARDENS

One of the wonderful things about gardening is that it's always unfinished. There are always new things to plant, more work to be done, and fresh innovations to implement. Besides the planting, growing, and other things associated with plants, flowers, and herbs themselves, there are all sorts of DIY projects you can take on.

ELEVATED GARDEN PLANTER

Raised garden boxes are perfect for anyone with limited space because they let you grow several plants on decks, on patios, or in small yards while solving most of the common gardening headaches. You can fill the boxes with exactly the right soil that your plants need instead of dealing with whatever soil is already in your yard, and the water drains properly, so your plants won't get waterlogged roots. Plus, since the boxes are raised, you won't have to bend over constantly when watering or harvesting, making gardening much more comfortable, enjoyable, and accessible.

Raised garden boxes act like protective barriers that keep most bugs and weeds away from your plants, so you'll spend less time fighting pests and pulling weeds. When bad weather hits, you can easily cover the boxes or even move smaller ones to more sheltered spots. The neat, organized look of raised boxes makes your space feel bigger and more intentional rather than cluttered and messy. Finally, the soil warms up faster in the spring compared to ground-level gardens, which means you can start planting earlier and keep growing vegetables later into the fall, leading to a longer harvest season even in tight spaces.

Materials and Cut List
LUMBER

- Two pieces measuring $5/4$in x 6in x 8ft
- Two pieces measuring 2in x 2in x 8ft
- One piece measuring 1in x 6in x 6ft

HARDWARE, TOOLS, AND OTHER SUPPLIES

- Thirty-six 2-in deck screws
- Power Drill
- Saw
- Tape Measure
- Pencil
- Sandpaper

OPTIONAL BUT RECOMMENDED

- Fabric or plastic lining
- Paint or wood stain of your choice

LUMBER CUTS

- Legs, cut from the 2in x 2in x 8ft lumber
- Four pieces at 18in long
- Two crosspieces at 27in long
- Two crosspieces at $13\frac{1}{8}$in long
- Box components, cut from the $5/4$in x 6in x 8ft lumber
- Four pieces at 33in long
- Four pieces at 11in long
- Base, cut from the 1in x 6in x 6ft lumber
- Two pieces at 31in long

Step-by-Step Assembly
Step 1: Prepare the Legs

A Cut all leg pieces to their specified lengths.

B On the four 18-in leg pieces, mark 11in from one end. Pre-drill holes below the 11-in mark to prevent the wood from splitting.

1
2
2C
3A
3B
4

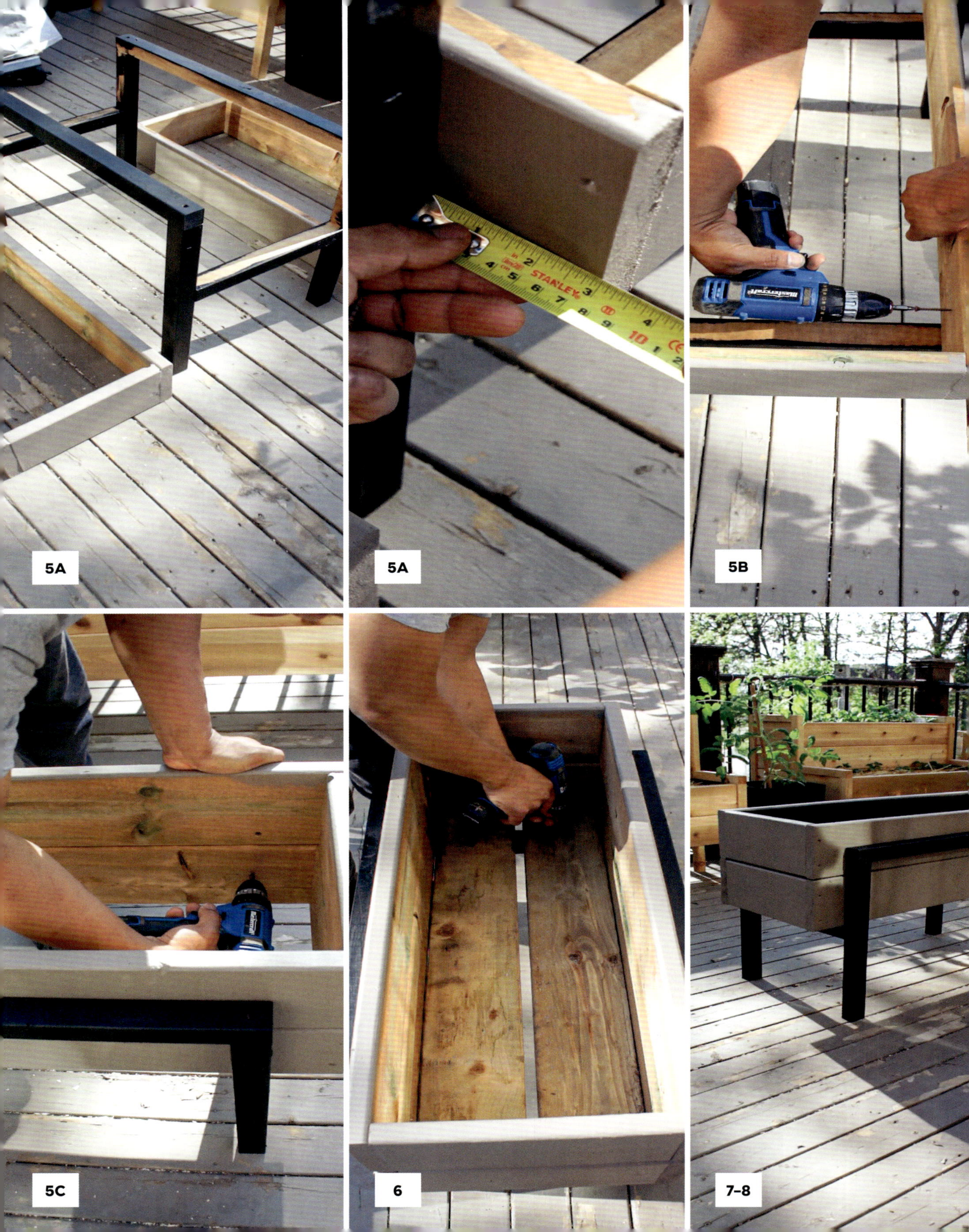

5A
5A
5B
5C
6
7-8

Step 2: Build the Leg-Support Structure

A Take two 18-in legs and position one 13⅛-in crosspiece horizontally between the two legs at the 11-in marks you made earlier.

B Secure with 2-in deck screws, ensuring the structure is square and stable, and repeat this process with the remaining two 18-in legs and 13⅛-in crosspiece.

C Connect the leg pairs with the two 27-in crosspieces on top, creating a stable frame.

Step 3: Construct the Lower Box

A Pre-drill holes in the corners of two of the ⁵⁄₄in x 6in x 33in pieces to prevent splitting.

B Assemble the pieces into a rectangular box using two ⁵⁄₄in x 6in x 33in pieces as the front and back, and two ⁵⁄₄in x 6in x 11in pieces as the ends.

C Secure all joints using 2-in deck screws, ensuring corners are square and joints are tight.

Step 4: Construct the Upper Box

A Repeat the same process with the remaining two ⁵⁄₄in x 6in x 33in pieces and two ⁵⁄₄in x 6in x 11in pieces to create a second identical rectangular box. Remember to pre-drill all screw holes to avoid wood splitting.

Step 5: Attach Boxes to Leg Structure

A Position the lower box on the leg structure so it rests on the 13⅛-in crosspieces. Center the box so there is a 3-in gap from the outside of each leg to the edge of the box on both sides.

B Secure with 2-in deck screws through the box sides into the legs. Important: Do not fully tighten the screws yet—just position securely.

C Position the upper box on top of the lower box. Secure the upper box with screws, checking for alignment and centered position.

Step 6: Install the Base

A Take the two 1in x 6in x 31in base pieces. Position them inside the lower box to create a floor.

B Screw the base pieces directly into the 13⅛-in crosspieces of the leg structure. Leave small gaps between the base boards for drainage.

Step 7: Final Assembly

A Once both boxes are positioned correctly, fully tighten all screws.

B Check that the structure is stable and square. Sand any rough edges or surfaces.

Step 8: Finishing Touches

A Add lining: Install fabric or plastic lining in the box to prevent soil spillage.

B Apply finish: If desired, apply wood stain or paint for weather protection.

C Create drainage: Ensure there are small gaps or holes for water drainage if installing a plastic lining.

HARVEST BASKET

As you might expect by its name, a harvest basket is a container used to store the lovely fruits, vegetables, and flowers you pick from your garden, enabling you to wash your beauties right after you gather them up. Here's an easy way to make a great one:

Materials and Cut List

LUMBER

- One piece of cedar fence board measuring 1in x 6in x 6ft (note that the actual board measures to about $\frac{5}{8}$in x $5\frac{1}{8}$in x 72in—lumber stores often list larger sizes than the actual size)

HARDWARE, TOOLS, AND OTHER SUPPLIES

- Fourteen 1-in screws
- $\frac{1}{2}$-in hardware cloth measuring 12in x 16in
- $\frac{3}{4}$-in wood dowel measuring 8in
- Saw
- Jigsaw
- Staple gun with $\frac{9}{16}$-in staples
- Wood glue
- Sandpaper
- Pencil
- Tape measure
- Hammer
- Drill
- $\frac{1}{8}$-in drill bit

LUMBER CUTS

- Two end pieces measuring $\frac{5}{8}$in x $5\frac{1}{8}$in x 8in
- Two side-rail pieces measuring $\frac{5}{8}$in x $2\frac{1}{2}$in x 16in
- Two handle-support pieces measuring $\frac{5}{8}$in x $1\frac{1}{2}$in x $7\frac{1}{4}$in

Step-by-Step Assembly

Step 1: Prepare the Wood Pieces

A Cut the wood pieces to size.

B Take the two $\frac{5}{8}$in x $5\frac{1}{8}$in x 8in end pieces and mark lines for radius cuts on the bottom corners of each. From the bottom of the side measuring $5\frac{1}{8}$in, mark at $1\frac{3}{4}$in. On the side measuring 8in, mark at $2\frac{1}{4}$in.

C Using any round object, such as a plastic lid, mark the radius and cut with a jigsaw.

D In the top corners of each end piece, cut a $\frac{5}{8}$in x $2\frac{1}{2}$in notch with a jigsaw.

E Pre-drill two $\frac{1}{8}$-in holes on the ends of the $\frac{5}{8}$in x $2\frac{1}{2}$in x 16in side rail pieces to prevent splitting.

F Pre-drill one hole on the top end of the $\frac{5}{8}$in x $1\frac{1}{2}$in x $7\frac{1}{4}$in handle support pieces for the dowel. Pre-drill two holes on the bottom end, centered and within $2\frac{1}{2}$in from the edge.

Step 2: Prepare the Side Rails

A Take the hardware cloth and make a 90-degree bend $\frac{1}{2}$in from the edge along the 16-in end. Repeat on the opposite edge.

B Using the staple gun, attach one of the bent edges of the hardware cloth to one of the side rails.

1B 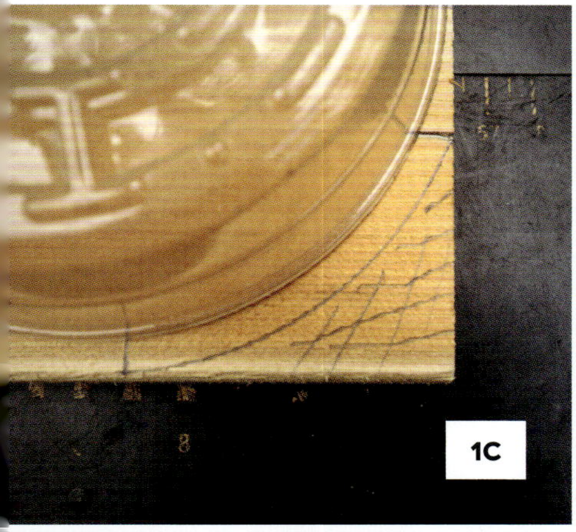
CurveControl™
1C 
1C–1D 
1E 
1E

2
3A
3A
3D
4B
4D

Step 3: Attach the Side Rails to the End Pieces

A Place one side rail in the notches on both end pieces. Add glue to the notches and screw in place.

B Wrap the hardware cloth around the end pieces, following the contour of the wood.

C Position the second side rail in the notches, drill holes, and screw in place.

D Use the staple gun and hammer to attach the hardware cloth to the bottom and sides of the end pieces.

Step 4: Attach the Handle Supports

A On each side of the side rails, mark 7½in and center the two handle-support pieces.

B Apply glue to the bottom end of the handle support and attach it to the side rail at the 7½-in mark. Screw in place and repeat on the opposite side.

C Apply glue to both ends of the dowel and attach it to the top of each handle support. Screw in place.

D After the glue has dried, sand the edges—and your basket is ready to use!

THREE-TIER WORM COMPOST BIN

Vermicomposting, or worm composting, is the process of using worms to convert food scraps, shredded paper, and other organic materials into compost, also known as worm castings. Worm castings are rich, organic soil amendments containing a diversity of plant nutrients and beneficial microorganisms.

Red wiggler worms are the best compost worms. They live within 6 inches of the topsoil, tend to move upward to where the food is, and rarely burrow deep underneath the soil. They are aggressive breeders and heavy eaters, helping decompose dead organic materials into humus, increasing the fertility of the soil and turning food waste into a rich source of fertilizer. Worm castings can go right into your garden and can be used very liberally. Start with a thin layer of manure, add the red wiggler worms, place organic materials on top, and then follow with paper shreds. Worms will eat their way up!

Materials and Cut List

LUMBER

- Four cedar pieces measuring 1in x 6in x 6ft (true size: ⅝in x 5⅛in x 72in)
- Four pine pieces measuring 1in x 2in x 8ft (true size: ⅝in x 1½in x 96in)
- Two pine pieces measuring 2in x 2in x 8ft (true size: 1½in x 1½in x 96in)

HARDWARE, TOOLS, AND OTHER SUPPLIES

- One wire mesh piece (¼in or ½in square, galvanized or plastic) measuring 3ft x 20in
- One fine mesh piece measuring 3in x 3in
- Two fine mesh pieces measuring 5in x 5in
- One piece of 6-mil polyethylene plastic measuring 24in x 16in
- Sixteen deck screws measuring 2½in
- Thirty-six deck screws measuring 1½in
- Power drill
- 3-in hole saw bit
- ⅛-in drill bit
- 1-in spade bit
- Miter saw or hand saw
- Wire cutter
- Tape measure
- Pencil
- Wood glue
- Hammer and 1-in nails if not using nail gun
- Staple gun and 9⁄16-in or ⅜-in staples
- Nail gun and 1¾6-in nails (optional)

LUMBER CUTS

- From the four cedar pieces measuring 1in x 6in x 6ft, cut:
  - Ten pieces at 20in long
  - Six pieces at 11in long
- From the four pine pieces measuring 1in x 2in x 8ft, cut:
  - Ten pieces at 20in long
  - Eight pieces at 13½in long
  - Three pieces at 5in long
- From the two pine pieces measuring 2in x 2in x 8ft, cut:
  - Two pieces at 17in long
  - Four pieces at 16in long
  - Two pieces at 9½in long
  - One piece at 5in long

Step-by-Step Assembly

<u>PART ONE: BUILD THREE BINS</u>

In this first part of the build, you'll be using the following lumber cuts and materials:

- Six pieces of cedar measuring ⅝in x 5⅛in x 20in
- Six pieces of cedar measuring ⅝in x 5⅛in x 11in
- Six pieces of pine measuring ⅝in x 1½in x 20in
- Six pieces of pine measuring ⅝in x 1½in x 13½in
- The wire mesh piece measuring 3ft x 20in
- Twenty-four 1½-in deck screws

Step 1: Pre-Drill

A Start with two cedar pieces measuring 5⅛in x 20in. From the edges of both, mark a guideline matching the thickness of the board, which should be about ⅝in.

B Using a ⅛-in drill bit, pre-drill two holes about 1in from the top and bottom corners and centered to the thickness of the board. This will prevent the wood from splitting when you screw the board in place.

Step 2: Make the Box

A Take two 5⅛in x 11in cedar boards and add glue on each end.

B Place each piece on both ends of one of the 5⅛in x 20in boards from Step 1 to create a rectangular box. Make sure the edges are flush and square, using a block to help square the edges.

C Using the 1½-in deck screws, drill in place slowly to avoid splitting the wood.

D Install a second 5⅛in x 20in cedar board on the opposite side. Check that the structure is stable and square.

Step 3: Install the Mesh

A From the galvanized or plastic-wire mesh measuring 3ft x 20in, cut three pieces measuring 20in x 12in.

B Use a staple gun and hammer to secure the wire mesh to the bottom of the box frame.

Step 4: Build the Outer Frame

A Mark 1in from the top of each corner of the box.

B Take one pine piece measuring 1½in x 20in and glue in place, lining up the bottom to the marked lines.

C Make sure the edges are flush, nail it in place (for easy installation, use a nail gun), and repeat on the other side.

D Next, take two pine pieces measuring 1½in x 13½in. Align it with the 1-in mark on the box, apply glue, and nail it down. Repeat on the other side.

Step 5: Repeat

A Simply repeat steps one through four to build two more bins!

Tip: For a smooth fitting, round off the bottom corners and edges using a sander.

Part 1:
1
Part 1:
2B
Part 1:
2C
Part 1:
3
Part 1:
2D
Part 1:
4A

Part 1:
4B

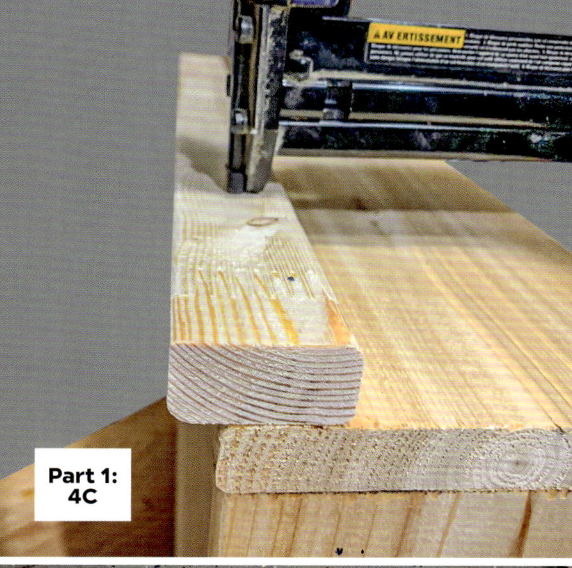
Part 1:
4C

Part 1:
4C

Part 1:
4D

Part 1:
5A

PART TWO: BUILD THE BASE

In part two, you'll be using the following lumber cuts and materials:

- Two cedar pieces measuring ⅝in x 5⅛in x 20in
- Three pine pieces measuring ⅝in x 1½in x 20in
- Two pine pieces measuring ⅝in x 1½in x 13½in
- Four pine pieces measuring 1½in x 1½in x 16in
- Two pine pieces measuring 1½in x 1½in x 17in
- Two pine pieces measuring 1½in x 1½in x 9½in
- One fine-mesh piece measuring 3in x 3in
- One piece of 6-mil polyethylene plastic measuring 24in x 16in
- Sixteen deck screws measuring 2½in
- Ten deck screws measuring 1½in

Step 1: Build the Leg Frames

A Take one pine piece measuring 1½in x 17in and apply glue to one end.

B Place one pine piece measuring 1½in x 16in on the end of the 17-in pine piece and join together with the 2½-in deck screws. You can either use 2 screws side by side in the center or 2 screws on opposite corners.

C Apply glue to the other end of the 17-in pine piece and screw in place another 16-in pine piece.

D Repeat this process to make two leg frames.

Step 2: Install the Leg Frames

A Apply glue to the two pine pieces measuring 1½in x 9½in and attach them to one of the leg frames from the previous step using the 2½-in deck screws. (Refer to image Part 2: 1B on page 142 for screw placement.)

B Attach the other leg frame.

Step 3: Make the Base

A Measure the top of the base for a total width of 12¼in. On both ends, install the cedar pieces measuring 5⅛in x 20in with the 1½in screws.

B Center a pine piece measuring 1½in x 20in and secure with deck screws. Note that there will be a gap, which will be covered with plastic.

Step 4: Add Drainage

A Create a drain hole at the bottom of the base using the 1-in spade bit.

B Cover the hole with the 3in x 3in fine mesh piece. Staple the mesh in place.

Step 5: Attach the Outer Frame

A Measure and mark 1in from the top of the base all around.

B Take the two 1½in x 20in pine pieces, apply glue, and install on both sides of the box with hammer and nails, aligning the bottom to the marked line and ensuring flush edges.

C Glue and install the remaining two 1½in x 13½in pine pieces. The inside width should measure 12¼in x 20in.

Step 6: Add the Plastic Cover

A Take the 24in x 16in piece of 6-mil polyethylene plastic, center it over the frame, and staple it from the top corner all the way around. As you staple, push the plastic downward.

B Fold the corners and cut a hole over the drainage hole. Secure the drainage hole with staples.

Tips

- Make sure to place a bucket underneath if you're storing the bin indoors.
- Place your bins on level ground to prevent water overspill.

Part 2:
1B

Part 2:
1B

Part 2:
2A

Part 2:
2B

Part 2:
Step 3

Part 2:
4A

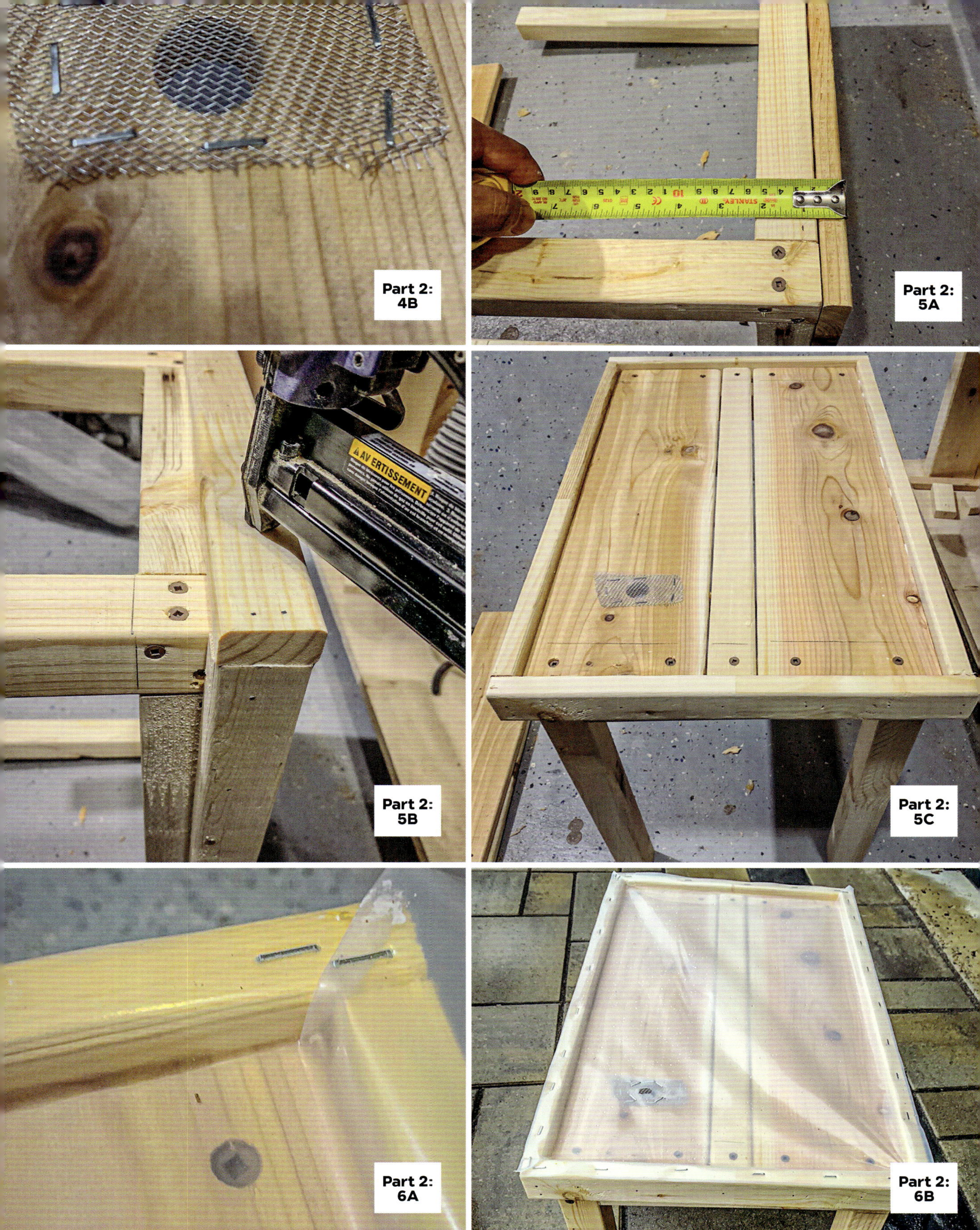

Part 2:
4B

Part 2:
5A

AV ERTISSEMENT
Part 2:
5B

Part 2:
5C

Part 2:
6A

Part 2:
6B

PART THREE: BUILD THE LID

For part three, you'll be using the following lumber cuts:

- Two cedar pieces measuring ⅝in x 5⅛in x 20in
- One pine piece measuring ⅝in x 1½in x 20in
- Three pine pieces measuring ⅝in x 1½in x 5in
- One pine piece measuring 1½in x 1½in x 5in
- Two pieces of fine mesh measuring 5in x 5in
- Two deck screws measuring 1½in

Step 1: Make the Lid

A Take the two cedar pieces measuring 5⅛in x 20in and align the pine piece measuring 1½in x 20in in the middle. Ensure the edges are flush and tighten close together.

B Next, take the three 1½in x 5in pine pieces. Apply glue to one side of one piece. Position it perpendicular to the boards, centered on the underside of the lid, and nail it in place.

C Glue and nail down the two remaining 1½in x 5in pieces perpendicular to the boards at the top and bottom ends, leaving 2in of space inward from the short edges. These create the lip that allows the lid to sit on the box.

Step 2: Add Air Holes

A Take one of the three bins you've constructed, and place the lid on top. Using the 3-in hole saw bit, drill two holes on opposite ends, leaving 1in of room at the edge. (If you don't have a hole saw, simply use a standard drill, and drill a few holes on each end.)

B Place the two 5in x 5in fine-mesh pieces over the holes, and staple in place.

Step 3: Make the Handle

A Flip over the lid and center the 1½in x 1½in x 5in handle piece lengthwise. Mark its position on both ends and pre-drill two holes through the lid at each marked location.

B Apply glue to the bottom of the 1½in x 1½in x 5in handle piece and position on the marks. Flip the lid back over and secure using two 1½-in deck screws at each end.

Voilà! Now you have a brag-worthy worm-composting bin. Although this project has many steps, it'll be worth the time and energy. It's inexpensive and easy to maintain—and it'll supercharge your soil and plants for years to come.

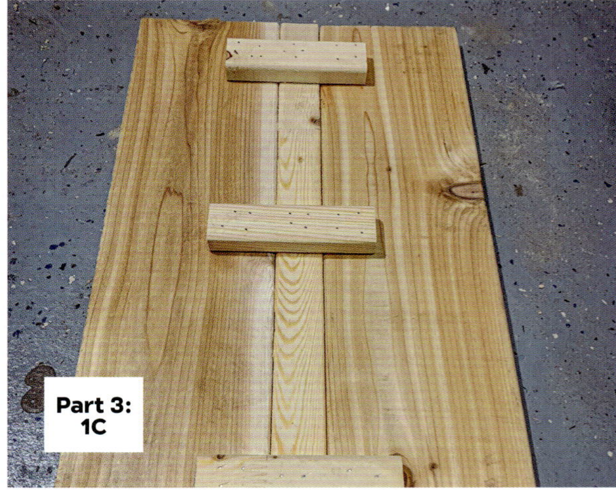

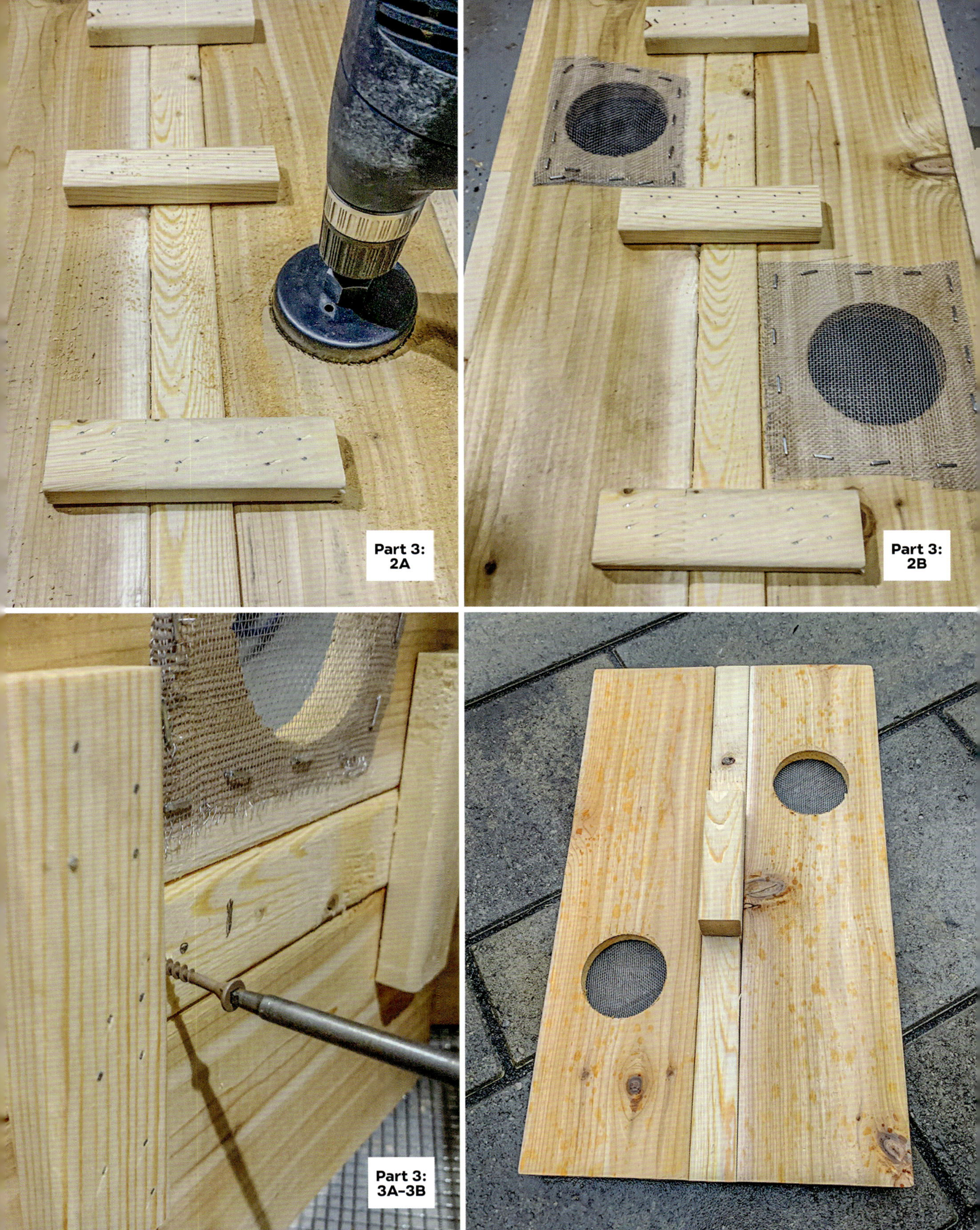

Part 3:
2A

Part 3:
2B

Part 3:
3A–3B

MULTI-GARLIC DIBBLER

This multi-garlic dibbler design allows you to plant eight garlic cloves simultaneously with perfect 6-in spacing and consistent 4-in depth. It's a game-changer for larger garlic plantings.

Materials List

- One piece of pine or cedar board measuring 1in x 10in x 23in
- Eight 1-in wood dowels measuring 4½in long
- Wood glue
- Sandpaper (120 and 220 grit)
- Drill and 1-in spade bit
- Tape measure
- Pencil
- Eight 1¼-in screws

Step-by-Step Assembly

Step 1: Prepare the Base Board

A Sand the board, starting with 120 grit and finishing with 220 grit. Mark 1in on all sides of the board and draw straight lines to connect.

B Starting from the left side of the top line, mark 8in and 15in, then repeat on the bottom line.

C Double-check that the spacing is marked as follows from the starting end: 1in, 8in, 15in, 22in. These marks are the centers for each dowel.

Step 2: Drill the Dowel Holes

A Using a 1-in spade bit, drill straight down at each mark, drilling ½in deep. For consistency, use painter's tape to mark the spade bit. To keep the holes perpendicular, use a drill press if available, or a drill guide.

B Next, test-fit the dowels—they should fit snugly but not require excessive force to push in.

C Clean the holes by removing all the wood chips and debris.

Step 3: Assembly

A Take one dowel and mark 4in from one end with a pencil, then insert all the dowels to check that the alignment is accurate.

B Apply a small amount of wood glue in each hole and insert the dowels. Check the alignment once more.

C Flip over the board and screw each dowel in place.

D Lastly, let the glue cure for 24 hours for full strength.

How to Use the Multi-Garlic Dibbler

A Loosen the top soil where you plan on planting.

B Position the dibbler over the planting area, then push straight down until the board touches the soil surface.

C Twist slightly to help create clean holes and prevent sticking. Then lift straight up—avoid any angling so as to maintain hole integrity.

D Drop one garlic clove in each hole, pointed end up.

E Push the soil back over the holes, and you're done! You can also flip over the tool and use it to flatten the surface of the soil.

COVERED GARDEN BED

This covered garden bed offers the perfect solution for extending your growing season and protecting your plants from unpredictable weather and unwanted pests. The combination of a sturdy raised bed with a removable hoop-house cover creates an ideal microclimate that can extend your gardening season by weeks or even months. During summer months, simply switch the plastic door covers with mesh netting for ventilation while maintaining protection from pests.

Materials and Cut List

LUMBER

- Four pieces measuring 2in x 12in x 12ft (for raised bed sides)
- Ten pieces measuring 2in x 2in x 8ft (for frame construction)
- Sixteen nailing strips measuring 1in x 1in x 4ft (for door frames)

HARDWARE, TOOLS, AND OTHER SUPPLIES

- 6-mil polyethylene plastic sheeting (clear or greenhouse grade)
- Ninety-five Kreg pocket screws (2½in recommended)
- Forty 2½-in wood screws (for frame joints)
- Fifty-two 1¼-in wood screws (for door frame)
- Staple gun and staples or clips for plastic attachment
- Wood glue (exterior grade)
- Kreg jig (pocket hole jig)
- Circular saw or miter saw
- Drill/driver
- Tape measure
- Sandpaper
- Square
- Level

LUMBER CUTS

- Frame components, cut from the 2in x 2in x 8ft boards
  - Three pieces at 25½in long, with a 45-degree cut on one end
  - Three pieces at 24in long, with a 45-degree cut on one end
  - Two pieces at 47¼in long (for ridge beam)
  - Two pieces at 8ft long (for base rails)
  - Three pieces at 33in long (two for base rails, one for center brace)
  - Two pieces at 24½in (for intermediate supports)
  - Four pieces at 4ft long (for corner braces)
  - Four pieces at 22in long (for inside corner reinforcements)
- Door frame components, cut from the 1in x 1in x 4ft nailing strips
  - Eight pieces at 47¾in long (for horizontal door frame)
  - Eight pieces at 27in long (for vertical door frame)
  - Twelve pieces at 4in long for door support
  - Twelve pieces at 3in long for door lock
- Bed side components, cut from the 2in x 12in x 12ft boards
  - Four pieces at 8ft long
  - Four pieces at 33in long

Step-by-Step Assembly

PART ONE: BUILD THE RAISED BED FRAME

Step 1: Cut the Bed Sides

Cut the bed side components to size according to the cut list. Sand all the cut edges smooth.

Step 2: Pre-Drill Pocket Holes

For the first two 2in x 12in x 8ft pieces, drill three 2½-in pocket holes on the inside faces on each 12-in end. Follow the same process for the first two 2in x 12in x 33in pieces. For the remaining two 2in x 12in x 8ft pieces, drill three pocket holes on each end, plus five pocket holes along one long side. For the remaining two 33-in pieces, drill three pocket holes on each end, plus two pocket holes along one long side.

Step 3: Secure the Bed Side Pieces

Stack two 2in x 12in x 8ft pieces on top of each other. Place a piece with pocket holes on the long side on top of a piece without long-side pocket holes, then attach them together using 2½-in pocket screws to create one 2in x 24in x 8ft piece. Repeat with the remaining 8-ft pieces. Then repeat the entire process for both of the 2in x 12in x 33in pieces to create two 2in x 24in x 33in pieces.

Step 4: Attach the Corner Braces

Take one 2in x 24in x 8ft bed side and attach one 2in x 2in x 4ft corner brace to each end (ensuring it's flush with the bottom) with wood glue, followed by 2½-in pocket screws. Repeat with the second 2in x 24in x 8ft bed side, attaching the remaining two corner braces. Stand the 2in x 24in x 33in pieces vertically and attach them to the free ends of the corner braces using wood glue and pocket screws. Attach the remaining 2in x 24in x 8ft piece with the corner braces to complete the rectangular bed frame.

Step 5: Reinforce the Corners

Attach the four 22-in corner-reinforcement pieces to the inside corners of the bed side frame using 2½-in wood screws to create a strong, rigid corner connection. Then attach the 33-in center-brace piece to the middle of the 8-ft bed sides to prevent the middle from bowing. Check for squareness using a tape measure (diagonals should be equal).

PART TWO: ASSEMBLE THE COVER FRAME

Step 1: Install Base Rails

Attach two 2in x 2in x 8ft base rail pieces to the top ends of the 2in x 2in x 4ft corner braces. Then attach two 2in x 2in x 33in base rail pieces to the remaining short sides of the top 4-ft corner braces. Use pocket screws and wood glue for secure attachment.

Step 2: Add Intermediate Supports

Install the 24½-in intermediate supports between the 8-ft bed sides and 8-ft base rails. Position it to the center—each side should have 47¼in of spacing.

Step 3: Build the End Triangles

To create the three triangular end frames, use the Kreg jig to drill pocket holes on the straight end of the 24-in pieces. Connect the 25½-in and 24-in pieces at their straight cuts to form an L shape for the peak. Use wood glue and 2½-in pocket screws for strong joints. The base of each triangle should measure approximately 36in. Attach the bottoms of the triangles to the 33-in base rails, two on each end and one at the center of the 8-ft base rails,

Part 1:
Step 1

Part 1:
Step 2

Part 1:
Step 2

Part 1:
Step 2

Part 1:
Step 3

Part 1:
Step 4

Part 1:
Step 4

Part 1:
Step 4

Part 1:
Step 5

Part 1:
Step 5

Part 2:
Step 1

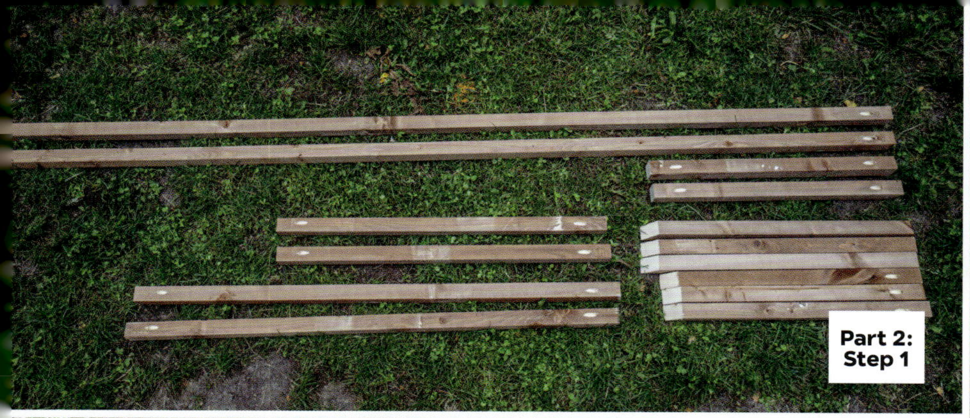
Part 2: Step 1

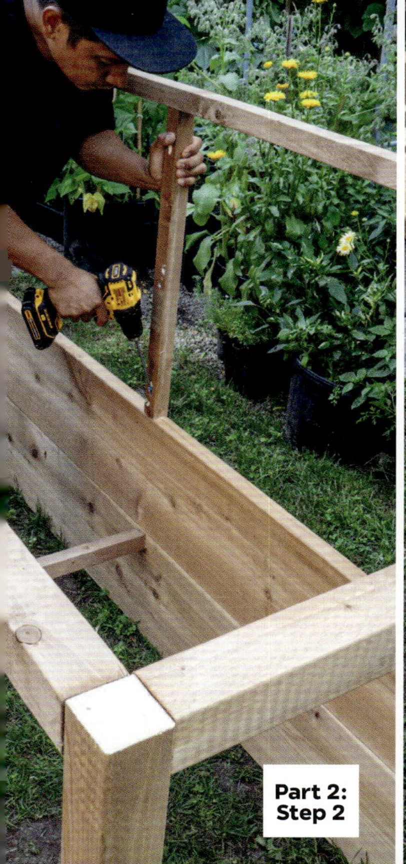

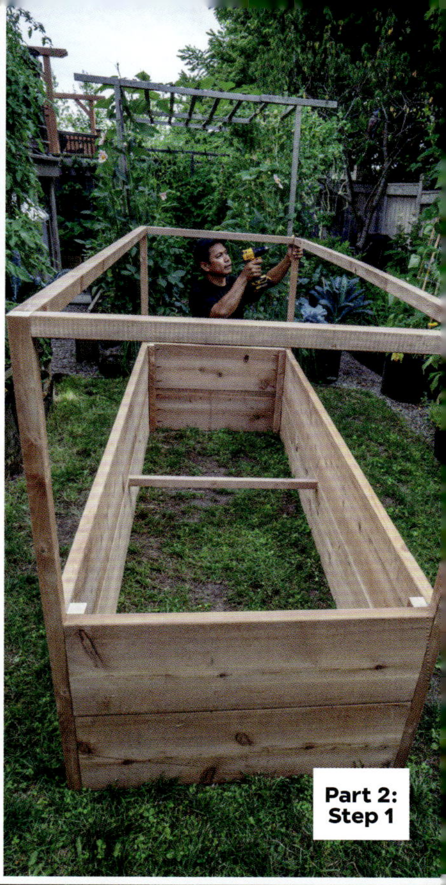
Part 2: Step 1

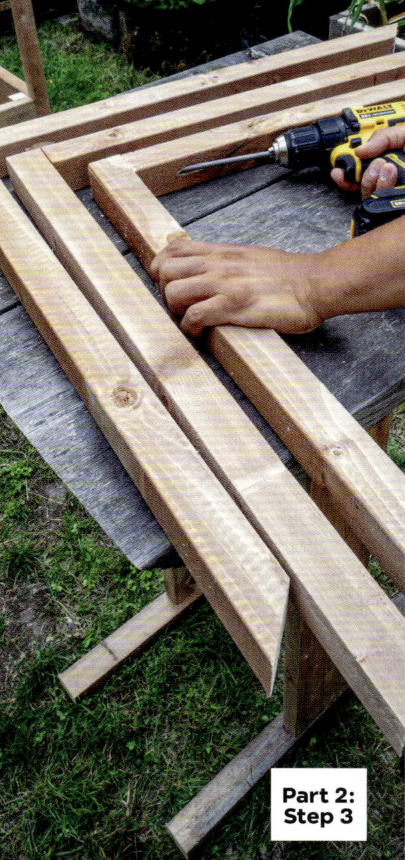

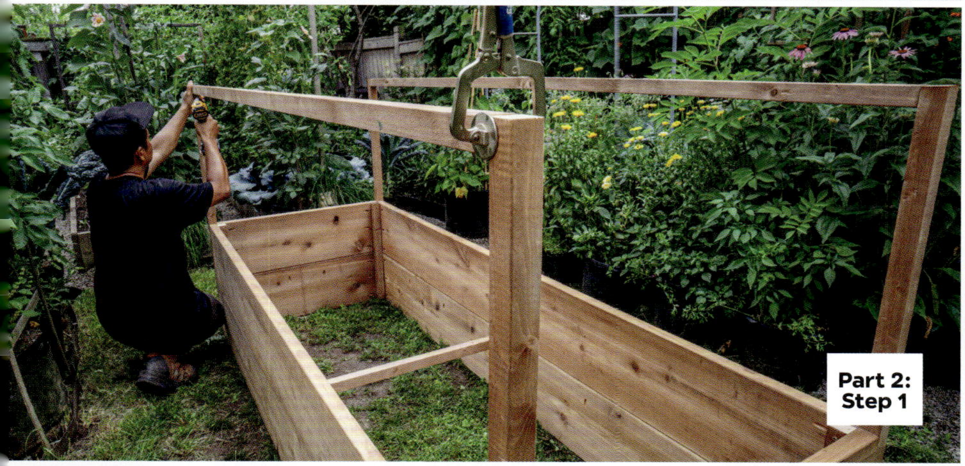
Part 2: Step 1

Part 2: Step 2

Part 2: Step 3

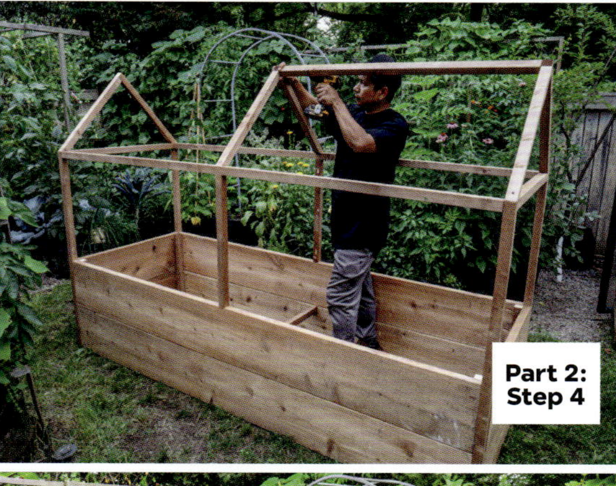

Part 2: Step 4

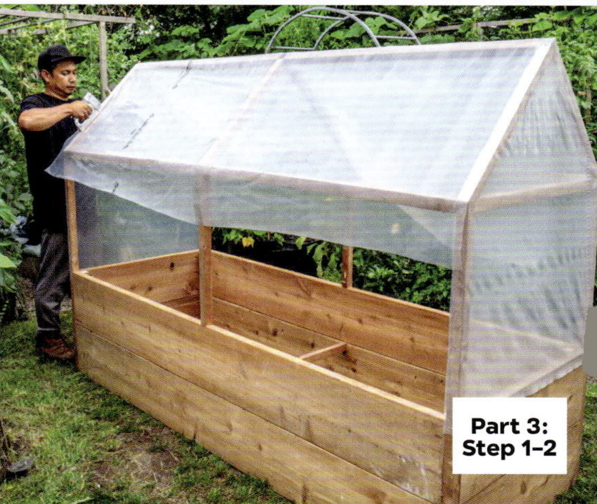

Part 3: Step 1–2

Part 4:
Step 1
Part 4:
Step 1
Part 4:
Step 2
Part 4:
Step 3
Part 4:
Step 3
Final
Assembly

aligned with the intermediate supports. Use wood glue and 2½-in wood screws to secure in place.

Step 4: Install the Ridge Beam

Connect the two 47¼-in ridge beam pieces at the peak. Use the Kreg jig for clean pocket hole connections, and check to ensure the structure is square and level.

PART THREE: INSTALL PLASTIC COVERING

Step 1: Measure and Cut the Plastic

Measure the frame to determine the plastic size needed and add 6 to 8in of extra space on all sides to allow for a secure attachment. Cut the 6-mil polyethylene plastic to size. Tip: Choose a calm day for installation to prevent wind issues.

Step 2: Attach the Plastic Covering

Starting at one end, stretch the plastic over the frame, pulling taut but not overly tight to allow for thermal expansion. Secure with heavy-duty staples every 6 to 8in along the frame. Work systematically around the entire structure and trim excess plastic, leaving 2in from the edge of the frame for weatherproofing.

PART FOUR: BUILD REMOVABLE ACCESS DOORS

Step 1: Assemble the Door Frames

Create four rectangular door frames using the 47¾-in and 27-in door-frame pieces, two for the front and two for the back. Each frame should measure 48½in wide by 27in tall. Use wood glue and 1¼-in screws at the corners, and pre-drill to prevent splitting the nailing strips. Check each frame for squareness using diagonal measurements. Allow the glue to cure completely.

Step 2: Cover the Door Frames with Plastic

Cut four polyethylene plastic pieces for each door, measuring 54½in x 33in (which allows a 3-in overlap on all sides). Stretch the plastic over the back side of each door frame and staple down every 4 to 6in. Pull the plastic taut but be sure to allow slight flexibility. Trim the excess plastic, leaving a ½in beyond the staples.

Step 3: Install Removable Door Frames

Position the doors against the front and back openings of the main structure. Mark the door base support and lock locations. Use the 4-in and 3-in nailing strips to create several wooden locks. Pre-drill holes to prevent the wood from splitting. On each 8-foot long side of the bed frame, install six base supports measuring 4in and six wooden door locks measuring 3in. Place four supports at the ends (two at the top and bottom of each door frame ends) and two in the middle where the door frames meet. Position the six wooden locks to align with the base supports, with four at the ends and two in the middle. Repeat this installation process on the opposite side of the bed frame.

Final Assembly Tips

· Verify all joints are tight and secure.
· Check that the structure is square and level.
· Ensure the plastic is properly tensioned.
· Test stability by gently pushing on the frame.

SHADE NETTING

Easily install shade fabric to keep your plants protected from pests and harsh sunny days. It comes in different ranges of UV ray blocks, from 30 percent up. We added sticks on both ends to make it easier to move around and install. The shade we got fits all our 8-foot-long beds. It's really great for those hot, sunny days. We also use this netting to protect our garlic beds in the winter, preventing squirrels from digging up the cloves.

Using a staple gun is a quick and effective way to attach shade fabric to a wooden stick or pole. Here's how to do it properly:

Materials and Cut List

- Shade fabric (UV blocking fabric, 30 percent or higher). Length: 8ft (to match bed length) Width: As needed for your bed width + extra for folding edges. **Tip:** Measure your beds and add 2ft to the width for overhang on each side.
- Two wooden sticks or poles. Length: 8ft each. Diameter: ¾-in to 1-in thick (thin enough for easy handling but sturdy). Material: Untreated wood, bamboo poles, or lightweight wooden dowels.

HARDWARE, TOOLS, AND OTHER SUPPLIES

- Heavy-duty staples (¼-in to ⅜-in long)
- Staple gun

Step-by-Step Assembly

Step 1: Preparation

Choose heavy-duty staples (usually ¼-in to ⅜-in long) that can penetrate the fabric and bite well into the wood without going completely through the thin poles. Make sure your fabric edge is cut cleanly to prevent fraying.

Step 2: Basic Stapling Method

Fold the fabric edge over the stick by 1 to 2in to create a double layer—this prevents tearing and gives a cleaner look. Pull the fabric taut and staple along the fold every 3 to 4in. Keep steady pressure on the fabric while stapling to maintain consistent tension.

1
2
3
4
5
6

STRING TRELLIS

Sometimes the best solutions are the simplest ones. This traditional string trellis combines old school methods that are budget friendly, creating a reliable support structure for peas, cucumbers, beans, and other climbing vegetables. The beauty of twine lies in its versatility—beyond trellises, you'll find yourself reaching for it to stake tomatoes, bundle herbs, and tackle dozens of other garden tasks throughout the season.

While jute remains a popular choice, we've found that 100 percent cotton butcher twine offers distinct advantages. It's naturally strong and biodegradable, breaking down harmlessly in your compost when the time comes. The fact that it's food-safe means you can use the same roll in your kitchen for trussing roasts or tying herb bundles. Best of all, a 100-foot roll of this thick, durable twine costs less than $5—a small investment that will serve you for years to come.

Materials List
- Wooden or metal posts (vertical)
- Wooden or metal posts (horizontal, for top and bottom)
- Eyehooks (if using wooden posts)
- Allen key and drill (for wooden posts)
- Cotton butcher twine or jute (100-ft roll)
- Scissors

Step-by-Step Assembly

Step 1: Set up your frame. Install vertical posts with horizontal posts attached at the top and bottom to create a sturdy frame.

Step 2: Install the eyehooks. Place eyehooks 5in apart along both the horizontal posts (top and bottom) and the vertical posts. Use an Allen key attached to a drill to tighten the hooks fast. Note: Skip this step if using metal posts—you'll tie the string directly to them.

Step 3: Create the horizontal strings. Tie your twine horizontally across the posts, securing each end to the eyehooks (or directly to metal posts). Work your way from bottom to top, using the 5-in spacing.

Step 4: Cut the vertical strings. Measure and cut vertical strings that run from top to bottom. Make them slightly longer than the measured height to allow for tying.

Step 5: Weave the vertical strings. Starting at the top, weave each vertical string by going under and over each horizontal string. This weaving pattern locks the vertical strings in place without requiring knots at every intersection.

Step 6: Secure the bottom. When you reach the bottom eyehook, tie the vertical string in a secure knot. Trim any excess tail ends.

Once complete, your trellis will provide years of reliable service with minimal maintenance. When the twine eventually starts to break down after years of use, simply cut it down and add it to your compost pile, where it will decompose naturally. The frame can be restrung in minutes, making this one of the most sustainable and cost-effective trellising solutions available to the home gardener.

MAINTAINING YOUR COMPACT GARDEN

If you've gotten this far, you probably already have some beautiful plants, flowers, or vegetables in your garden. Congratulations! Getting it established is the hard part. Now you need to know how to look after your homemade paradise. Sometimes even the most experienced gardeners are tempted to overlook this routine maintenance. But that's no more advisable than neglecting to brush your teeth twice daily or shower multiple times per week. Go too long without taking care of these basics, and you'll notice the effects of neglected health and hygiene. Similarly, your plants need a few things to continue living healthy and happy lives. Finally, you'll want to know how to harvest your beautiful bounty. Fear not: It's all in this chapter.

ROUTINE CARE AND MAINTENANCE

Bug check. Check plants you know are prone to pest attacks. Cucumber beetles, for example, like to hang around cucumber plants and squash flowers.

Harvesting. Morning is the best time to harvest vegetables, before the sun gets too hot. This helps to keep the vegetables fresh and prevents them from wilting.

Hand-pollinating. Hand pollination is using a small brush or cotton swab to transfer pollen from the male parts of a flower to the female parts when natural pollinators like bees aren't available. By hand-pollinating things like squash plants, you can assure better food production. If you notice you're not getting any fruits or you don't have bees or other pollinators present, then you probably want to use this technique. Hand-pollinating is essential for indoor gardening particularly, because there aren't any natural pollinators present inside.

Watering. Our garden has drip irrigation, but we still use our watering can for our greenhouse because it can get so hot during the day that additional daily watering is essential.

Hand pollinating squash increases harvest and guarantees fruit.

Pruning plants improves airflow and directs energy to fruit production.

TRIMMING AND PRUNING

Removing dead, damaged, or diseased branches reduces the risk of diseases spreading, prevents pests, and allows you to grow more food closer together due to improved light and airflow around the plants. When the foliage gets too heavy and the plant appears to be carrying too much weight, it's essential to prune.

Zucchini is a good example of the importance of pruning. Left unchecked, the large leaves can take up a lot of growing space and block pathways. You can prune the lower leaves, which take up energy from the plant, and grow zucchini vertically using a single stake and twist ties to support it. This not only gives you more room, but it also allows pollinators better access to flowers for more fruit production.

Conversely, not all types of tomatoes need to be pruned. Determinate tomatoes, which grow to a fixed mature size and ripen all their fruit within a few weeks, do not require pruning. However, indeterminate tomatoes, which produce fruit regularly over the course of a season, can benefit from selective pruning. Our preferred method is to prune the bottom leaves heavily because we grow tomatoes very close together. In our case, pruning improves air circulation around the plant, reducing the chances of moisture-related diseases and potential pest attacks. By removing excess growth, pruning also redirects the plant's energy back to the fruits, resulting in increased fruit production.

Pruning Guide

Why Prune? Better airflow, larger fruit, healthier plants

Tomatoes: Remove suckers, trim lower leaves

Peppers: Pinch first flowers for bushier growth

Cucumbers/Squash: Remove yellow leaves, trim non-fruiting vines

Beans/Peas: Pinch tips to encourage branching

Eggplants: Remove lower leaves, keep 5 to 6 main branches

Zucchini: Cut large shading leaves, remove old growth

Melons: Pinch vine tips after 4 to 5 fruits have set

Pumpkins: Limit to 2 to 3 fruits per vine, trim excess runners

Brussels Sprouts: Remove lower leaves as sprouts develop, top plant in late summer

Indeterminate Tomatoes: Prune to 1 to 2 main stems for larger fruit

Leafy Greens (Kale, Chard): Harvest outer leaves, remove flower stalks

Herbs (Basil, Mint): Pinch tops regularly, remove flower buds

TIPS

• Use clean, sharp tools
• Prune in dry weather
• Cut at a 45-degree angle
• Max 25 percent at once

TROUBLESHOOTING: Frequently Asked Questions

What's the difference between top dressing and side dressing in gardening?

Top dressing spreads fertilizer directly on the soil surface around the plants. Side dressing applies fertilizer in a shallow trench alongside plant rows, 4 to 6 inches from the stems. Both methods feed plants during the growing season without disturbing roots.

Why are my plant leaves turning yellow?

Yellow leaves can mean you're giving your plants too much water. It can also mean they need additional nutrients like nitrogen or that they have pests. Check the soil to see if it's too wet, and think about using a fertilizer like blood meal for added nitrogen.

What causes brown spots on leaves?

Brown spots might be from fungal infections, sunburn, or water left on leaves in the sun. Water your plants properly, and remove any leaves that look bad and keep them away from your garden or compost pile.

How do I get rid of aphids?

Use insecticidal soap to kill aphids and invite in ladybugs, which eat aphids and help keep them away.

How can I create a no-waste garden?

Compost plant scraps and kitchen waste, such as coffee grounds, to enrich soil. Save seeds from healthy plants, repurpose containers, and use grass clippings or leaves as mulch.

Why are my flowers not blooming?

If your flowers aren't blooming, it might be because they're not getting enough sunlight, they need more nutrients, or they've been pruned incorrectly. Make sure your plants have enough light, and consider using bone meal for added nutrients to encourage flowering.

What can I do about powdery mildew?

To fight powdery mildew, remove infected leaves, improve airflow around the plants, and apply natural treatments, like a mix of water with baking soda as a homemade spray.

Why is my mulch bringing in bugs?

Mulch creates a moist environment that attracts insects, but living mulch like pepper-carrot combinations won't harbor pests the way wood chips or straw do. Maintain plant spacing, water at the base, and remove diseased material promptly.

How do I choose the right container size for plants?

Match container size to root depth: shallow-rooted plants like lettuce and herbs need 6–8 inches, while deep-rooted crops like tomatoes and peppers require 12–18 inches. Ensure proper drainage holes to prevent root rot.

How can I tell if my soil is too acidic?

You can check the soil's pH level with a store-bought soil test kit. If it's below 6.5, it's acidic. You can add Dolomite lime to raise the pH in these cases.

Covering bare soil locks in moisture during hot summer months.

What should I do if my plants are leggy?

Leggy plants, which look tall and weak, usually need more light. Move them to a brighter spot or use grow lights.

How do I encourage more fruiting in my plants?

Make sure your plants get enough sunlight, water, and nutrients. Use fertilizers that are high in phosphorus and potassium. Pruning can also help focus energy on making fruit.

Why are my plants wilting despite watering?

Wilting can happen due to root rot from overwatering, root damage, or extreme heat. Check soil moisture, ensure proper drainage, and provide shade during peak sun exposure.

How can I keep squirrels from eating my fruits?

Use nets, cages, or repellents to keep squirrels away. You can also use shiny objects to scare them off and provide water bowls for thirsty squirrels that often damage fruits when they're just seeking moisture.

What can I do about snails and slugs?

You can pick them off by hand at night or set traps. Diatomaceous earth and copper barriers can also help keep them away.

How do I improve soil quality?

Add organic matter like compost or aged manure. Rotating crops regularly helps keep soil healthy too.

Why won't my seeds germinate?

Seeds need proper depth, moisture, and temperature to germinate. Plant at correct depth, keep soil moist, ensure temperatures are 65 to 75°F (18°C to 24°C), and check seed viability.

How do I deal with plants that are heavy feeders?

Heavy feeders like squash, melons, and tomatoes deplete soil quickly, so pair them with light feeders such as beans, peas, and herbs. Beans and peas add nitrogen back to the soil, making them ideal companions.

How do I attract pollinators to my garden?

Plant a variety of flowers and avoid using pesticides. Include native plants and provide water sources for them.

How should I position tall plants in my garden?

Plant tall crops like corn, sunflowers, pole beans, peas, trellised tomatoes, squash, melons and cucumbers on the north side to avoid blocking sunlight. Use their shade for shade-tolerant crops like lettuce, kale, and spinach.

How do I start a compost pile?

Pick a dry, shady spot and layer green materials (like vegetable scraps) and brown materials (like leaves). Turn the pile regularly and keep it moist.

How much light do my indoor plants need?

High-light plants, such as herbs, microgreens, and tomatoes, need south-facing windows. Leafy greens do well in east- or west-facing windows, while sprouts and mushrooms tolerate north-facing spots best. Plants that stretch toward the light need more sun, whereas scorched leaves indicate they're getting too much.

HARVESTING: Frequently Asked Questions

When is the best time to harvest vegetables?
The best time to pick vegetables is usually in the morning when the temperatures are cooler—it keeps the vegetables fresh and tasty.

How can I tell when my vegetables are ripe?
Each type of vegetable has its own signs that it's ripe. For example, tomatoes should have a deep color and feel a little soft when you touch them. On the other hand, cucumbers should be firm and have a bright green color.

What tools do I need for harvesting?
A sharp knife or scissors can help with cutting the vegetables. You will also need a basket or container to collect the vegetables. If you want to protect your hands, you might want to wear gloves.

How do I harvest leafy greens like lettuce?
You can cut and harvest the outer leaves at the base of the plant. This way, the inner leaves can keep growing.

Should I wash vegetables immediately after harvesting?

Some vegetables—such as leafy greens, carrots, beets, and radishes—can be washed right after harvest and stored clean. Potatoes and sweet potatoes, however, should be stored unwashed with the soil still on them. Tomatoes, berries, and other produce with a natural protective coating should be washed only just before use. If you wash vegetables before storing them, be sure to dry them thoroughly.

How often should I check for ripe vegetables?

Check on your vegetables regularly. Some, like zucchini and beans, may need to be checked every day. Others can be checked once a week.

What is the best way to pick vegetables without damaging the plant?

Gently twist the vegetable, or use clean pruning shears to cut it off. This helps keep the plant healthy.

Can I harvest vegetables if they're not fully mature?

Yes, you can pick some vegetables before they're fully grown. For instance, immature carrots and squash can be harvested early for a different taste. You can also pick tomatoes early if you have pests, like squirrels, eating them.

How do I store harvested vegetables?

After harvesting, you should store your vegetables in a cool, dry place, or in the refrigerator, depending on the type. For example, leafy greens should go in the fridge, while potatoes can be stored in a cool, dark room.

What should I do if I notice pests on my vegetables?

Check them closely and remove any parts that are affected. You can also wash the vegetables thoroughly to get rid of the pests.

How do I know if my root vegetables are ready to harvest?

You can harvest root vegetables like carrots and potatoes when they reach the size you want. For potatoes, you can tell they're ready when the leaves start to turn yellow.

How do I harvest herbs?

Cut off and harvest the top few inches of growth, which helps the plant grow bushier. Always cut above the leaf nodes and avoid cutting the woody part of the plant. For example, rosemary has a hard stem at the bottom and a greener part at the top.

What should I do with overripe vegetables?

If vegetables become overripe, you can either compost them or use them in cooking. However, it's important to remove them from the plant to stop any diseases from spreading.

Can I harvest vegetables in the rain?

It's best not to harvest vegetables during heavy rain. Wet conditions can lead to spoilage and make the vegetables more likely to get diseases.

How can I extend the shelf life of my harvested vegetables?

Store them properly and keep them in a cool, dark place. Use breathable bags to help extend their shelf lives.

CONCLUSION

Looking back on our journey, we started exactly where you might be now—with more enthusiasm than expertise, more questions than answers. Formal training isn't a prerequisite for creating something beautiful and productive. Our greatest teachers have been the seasons themselves: each mistake a lesson, each harvest a celebration. Your journey into small-space gardening doesn't end with the last page of this book. Instead, it's just beginning.

Think about what brought you here. Maybe you crave tomatoes that actually taste like summer, or maybe you want to live more sustainably right where you are. Whatever your reason, hold onto it—your "why" will be the compass that keeps you going when things get challenging. Every windowsill herb, balcony tomato, or vertical garden you tend to becomes a small act of optimism, a daily reminder that growth is always possible, no matter your space.

Remember, gardening is never about perfection. Some plants will thrive beyond your wildest hopes, while others will teach you lessons in patience and resilience. The wilted basil and the forgotten seedlings are just as much a part of your story as the abundant harvests. What matters is that you showed up, got your hands dirty, and helped nurture a living thing in your corner of the world.

Small-space gardening gives you permission to reimagine what's possible. In a world that often tells us we need more—more land, more space, more resources—you've proven that a little can go a long way. You've transformed overlooked spaces into sources of food, beauty, and joy. You've brought nature closer, even in the heart of the city.

So keep experimenting, keep growing, and keep celebrating every small victory. Your garden, no matter its size, is proof that anyone can be a gardener. And that's something worth cultivating.

PLANT, FLOWER, AND HERB PROFILES

For all the pleasure gardeners can take from gardening—being outdoors, getting your hands dirty in the earth, and so on—there is nothing as satisfying as growing the food you eat. The vegetables actually taste better when they're the product of your own hard work. Here are profiles for twenty of the most popular food plants, complete with details to help you maximize your efforts and grow the best produce you can. Keep in mind that this is information about the most ideal conditions, but it's very possible to cultivate plants in imperfect conditions. In addition, remember that some plants, like some people, are good together, sharing nutrients and helping each other grow. Others need to be kept apart. It's important to know the difference. We've also included profiles for nine of our favorite flowers and nine of our favorite herbs to grow alongside your veggies.

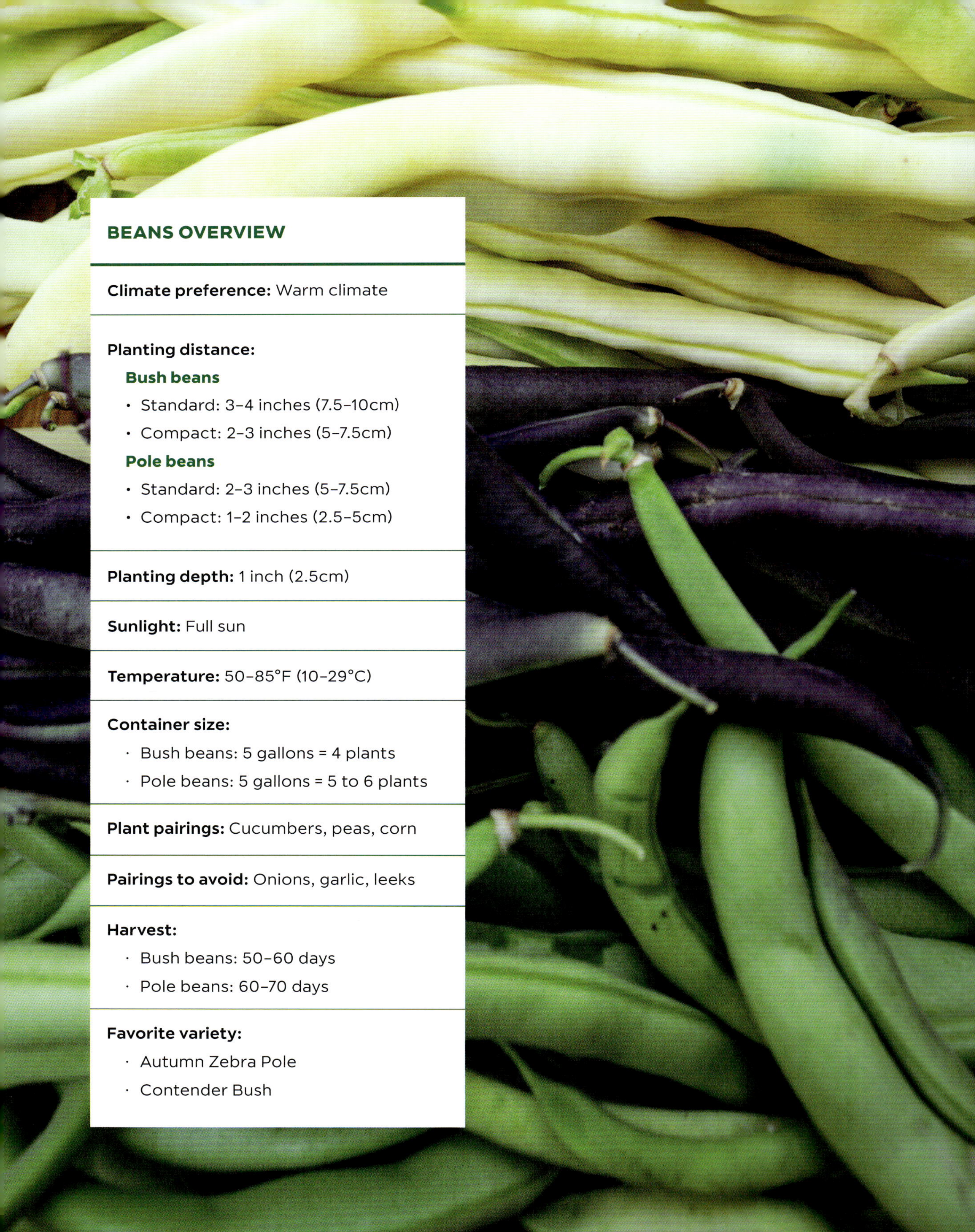

BEANS OVERVIEW

Climate preference: Warm climate

Planting distance:

Bush beans
- Standard: 3–4 inches (7.5–10cm)
- Compact: 2–3 inches (5–7.5cm)

Pole beans
- Standard: 2–3 inches (5–7.5cm)
- Compact: 1–2 inches (2.5–5cm)

Planting depth: 1 inch (2.5cm)

Sunlight: Full sun

Temperature: 50–85°F (10–29°C)

Container size:
- Bush beans: 5 gallons = 4 plants
- Pole beans: 5 gallons = 5 to 6 plants

Plant pairings: Cucumbers, peas, corn

Pairings to avoid: Onions, garlic, leeks

Harvest:
- Bush beans: 50–60 days
- Pole beans: 60–70 days

Favorite variety:
- Autumn Zebra Pole
- Contender Bush

PLANT PROFILES

BEANS

There are two main types: Bush beans are compact and grow quickly, while pole beans are climbers that need support, allowing for more beans in a smaller space and freeing up ground space for other plants.

Planting Beans 101

Beans are not frost-hardy and need soil temperatures of at least 50°F (10°C) to germinate, but they prefer temperatures between 60 and 70°F (15 and 21°C). It's best to plant them directly in soil with compost. Sow seeds 1 inch (2.5cm) deep. Space bush beans 3 to 4 inches (7.5 to 10cm) apart and pole beans 2 to 3 inches (5 to 7.5cm) apart. For a compact garden, bush beans can be planted 2 to 3 inches (5 to 7.5cm) apart, and pole beans 1 to 2 inches (2.5 to 5cm) apart—closer spacing can cause the plants to compete for nutrients.

Growing Beans 101

Beans need 6 to 8 hours of sunlight daily and do best in full sun, though they can handle part shade. Beans help enrich the soil by providing nitrogen, so you usually don't need to fertilize them, though we like to add a handful of compost. When the vines reach the top of the trellis, pinch off the top to encourage more branches and pods.

Growing Beans in Pots

Choose a pot at least 12 inches (30cm) deep. Water thoroughly and add compost every 4 to 6 weeks. In a 20-gallon container, plant 1 corn seedling in the middle surrounded by 4 to 6 bean plants. Beans climb the corn stalk for support, benefitting both crops.

Optional Amendments

- **Compost:** Mix into soil when you plant seeds.
- **Kelp meal:** Add at the start of the growing season.
- **Bone meal:** Best applied as soon as flowers start to appear.

Challenges

Common pests you might see include aphids, beetles, and slugs. Bring in helpful insects like ladybugs to manage aphids, and handpick beetles and slugs off the plants. You can also plant borage nearby to attract pests away from your main crops.

BEETS

Planting Beets 101

Beets love cool weather and are best sown directly. You can start planting them 4 to 6 weeks before the last frost using a cold frame. In warmer climates, plant them in the cooler months of fall or winter. Beets grow best in temperatures between 50 and 80°F (10 and 26°C). Choose a sunny spot, although they can handle some shade. The soil should be loose and well-draining; mix in compost or kelp meal to achieve this.

To plant beets, make a shallow trench about ½ inch (1cm) deep and plant seeds 2 to 3 inches (5 to 7.5cm) apart. In a small garden, you can plant them 1 inch (2.5cm) apart and harvest every other beet when they're small to let the others grow bigger, which is what we do to get two harvests in the same space. For larger beets, leave 3 to 4 inches (7.5 to 10cm) between plants. Cover the seeds lightly with soil, pat it all down, and water.

Growing Beets 101

Seeds should sprout in 7 to 14 days, depending on the temperature. Water 1 to 2 times per week. If the weather is hot or dry, you may need to water more often. As the plants grow, you might notice that some may be too close together, as seeds come in groups of 2 to 6 in each cluster so multiple plants may sprout in the same space. Gently pull out the smaller sprouts to give the bigger ones more room, aiming for 2 to 3 inches (5 to 7.5cm) between each plant. Beets like a little extra food, but it's not necessary—if you want, about 4 to 6 weeks in, add chicken-manure granules.

Growing Beets in Pots

Choose a container that's at least 10 to 12 inches (25 to 30cm) deep. Feed monthly with compost or chicken-manure granules. In a 5-gallon pot, plant 5 to 6 beets spaced 3 to 4 inches (7.5 to 10cm) apart.

Optional Amendments

- **Compost:** Mix in at planting stage and top off every few months.
- **Chicken-manure granules:** Apply a handful around the plant.
- **Bone meal:** Add in when planting.

Challenges

Avoid nitrogen-rich fertilizers, which lead to small roots and large leafy tops. Fungal diseases are caused by wet or humid soil. Ensure good drainage, avoid overwatering, and space plants out for adequate air circulation. Regularly check for pests like aphids, leaf miners, and flea beetles. Handpick bugs off the plants, and attract helpful insects like ladybugs.

BEETS OVERVIEW

Climate preference: Cool climate

Planting distance:
· Standard: 2–3 inches (5–7.5cm)
· Compact: 1 inch (2.5cm)

Planting depth: ½ inch (1cm)

Sunlight: Full sun, partial shade

Temperature: 50–75°F (10–24°C)

Container size:
· 5 gallons = 5 to 6 plants
· 10 gallons = 8 to 9 plants

Plant pairings: Onions, garlic, lettuce

Pairings to avoid: Swiss chard, pole beans

Harvest:
· Leaves: 35–45 days
· Roots: 50–70 days

Favorite variety:
· Early Wonder
· Chioggia

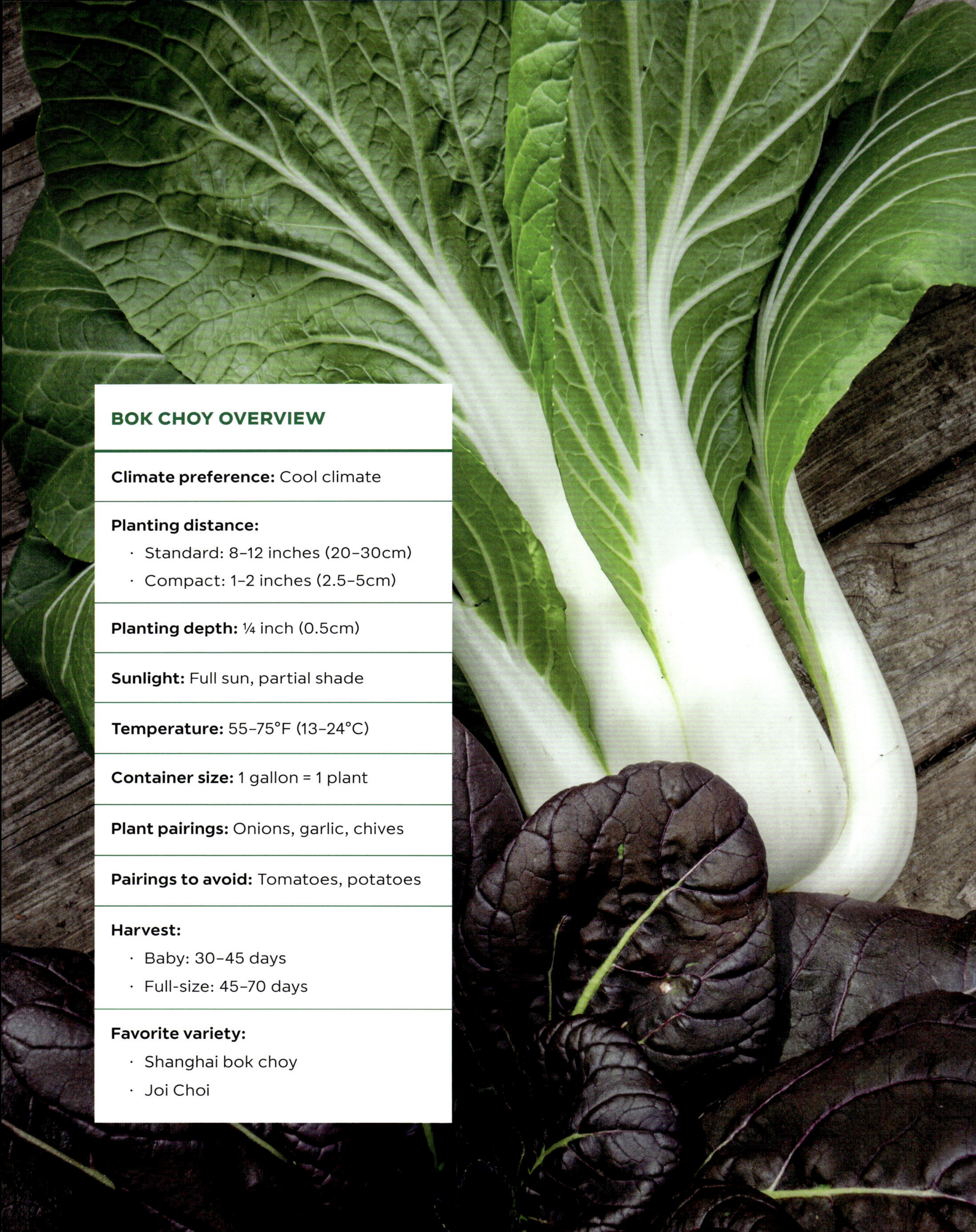

BOK CHOY OVERVIEW

Climate preference: Cool climate

Planting distance:
- Standard: 8–12 inches (20–30cm)
- Compact: 1–2 inches (2.5–5cm)

Planting depth: ¼ inch (0.5cm)

Sunlight: Full sun, partial shade

Temperature: 55–75°F (13–24°C)

Container size: 1 gallon = 1 plant

Plant pairings: Onions, garlic, chives

Pairings to avoid: Tomatoes, potatoes

Harvest:
- Baby: 30–45 days
- Full-size: 45–70 days

Favorite variety:
- Shanghai bok choy
- Joi Choi

BOK CHOY

Planting Bok Choy 101

Bok choy grows well in cooler weather, making it great for various climates, and grows well between 55 and 75°F (13 and 24°C). If it gets too hot, the vegetable can turn tough. In temperate climates, it's best to plant in early spring or late summer. In warm climates, you can grow it almost year-round, but it needs some shade during the hottest parts of the day. In cool climates, you can plant seeds directly (when soil is workable) or start indoors about 4 to 6 weeks before the last frost.

To plant bok choy, find a sunny spot, mix compost into the soil, sow the seeds about ¼ inch (0.5cm) deep, and cover them lightly with soil and water. Space the plants about 8 to 12 inches (20 to 30cm) apart for full growth or 1 to 2 inches (2.5 to 5cm) apart for baby leaves. If you started the seeds indoors, wait until they are 3 to 4 weeks old and have a few leaves before transplanting them to an outdoor garden. Bok choy grows quickly, fortunately.

Growing Bok Choy 101

Bok choy likes its soil to be consistently moist, so water 2 to 3 times per week. It also prefers full sun, needing about 4 to 6 hours of sunlight each day.

Growing Bok Choy in Pots

Choose a pot at least 8 to 10 inches (20 to 25cm) deep; a 1- to 3-gallon pot is ideal for 1 to 2 plants. Use potting mix for better drainage. Water deeply and use organic fertilizer every 2 to 3 weeks.

Optional Amendments

- **Compost:** Add before planting and top up every 3 to 4 weeks.
- **Fish emulsion:** Dilute fish emulsion with water and apply every 2 to 3 weeks.
- **Seaweed:** Use liquid seaweed fertilizer every 2 to 3 weeks.

Challenges

Common pests include aphids, slugs, and cabbage worms. Spray aphids off with a strong water stream, handpick slugs off the plants, and use row covers to stop moths from laying eggs. Prevent "bolting," which happens when plants flower too early, often due to heat, by planting in cooler weather, watering consistently, and providing shade during hot days.

BROCCOLI

Every time we tried to grow broccoli, our plants seemed to have other ideas. Instead of growing those luscious heads we craved, they decided to jump the gun and start bolting. Hot weather sent them into a flowering frenzy, and we were left with tiny clusters. Once we started timing it right, we could finally enjoy a full head of broccoli and even reap a second harvest of side shoots, like broccolini.

Planting Broccoli 101

Broccoli grows best in cool weather, thriving in spring and fall when temperatures are between 60 and 70°F (15 and 21°C). In warm climates, you can plant broccoli in fall for a winter harvest. In cool climates, you can plant seeds directly outdoors about 4 weeks before the last frost, or start them indoors 6 to 8 weeks before the last spring frost. Starting indoors usually gives better results. When planting broccoli seeds directly, choose a sunny spot with well-draining soil and compost. Plant seeds about ¼ to ½ inch (0.5 to 1cm) deep; standard spacing is 18 to 24 inches (45 to 60cm) apart since they grow large. Compact spacing is normally 12 to 15 inches (30 to 38cm) apart, but that may produce smaller heads. When transplanting outdoors, do it about 4 weeks before the last frost to get the plants used to outdoor conditions gradually.

Growing Broccoli 101

Broccoli loves moist soil, so water deeply 2 to 3 times per week. It's also a heavy feeder, meaning it needs plenty of nutrients to grow. Enrich the soil with natural amendments like compost, aged manure, or fish emulsion during the growing season. You can add fish emulsion or bone meal when you see a small head of broccoli forming.

Growing Broccoli in Pots

Choose a container that's at least 12 inches (30cm) deep and wide; generally, you'll want a 5- to 10-gallon container per plant. Place it in a sunny spot that gets at least 6 hours of sunlight daily.

Optional Amendments

- **Compost:** Add into the soil before planting and top dress every 4 to 6 weeks.
- **Fish emulsion:** Apply every 2 to 3 weeks.
- **Bone meal:** Add when planting and again when the broccoli heads begin to form.

Challenges

Common pests include cabbage worms, aphids, and flea beetles. Use row covers to protect the plants, and handpick pests when you see them. Plant broccoli in cooler months to prevent bolting and keep the soil consistently moist. Poor head development can occur from nutrient-deficient soil, so regularly amend the soil and feed your plants as needed.

BROCCOLI OVERVIEW

Climate preference: Cool climate

Planting distance:
· Standard: 18–24 inches (45–60cm)
· Compact: 12–15 inches (30–38cm)

Planting depth: ¼–½ inch (0.5–1cm)

Sunlight: Full sun, partial shade

Temperature: 60–70°F (15–21°C)

Container size: 5 gallons = 1 plant

Plant pairings: Beets, onions, garlic

Pairings to avoid: Tomatoes, eggplant

Harvest: 55–100 days

Favorite variety:
· Arcadia
· Waltham 29

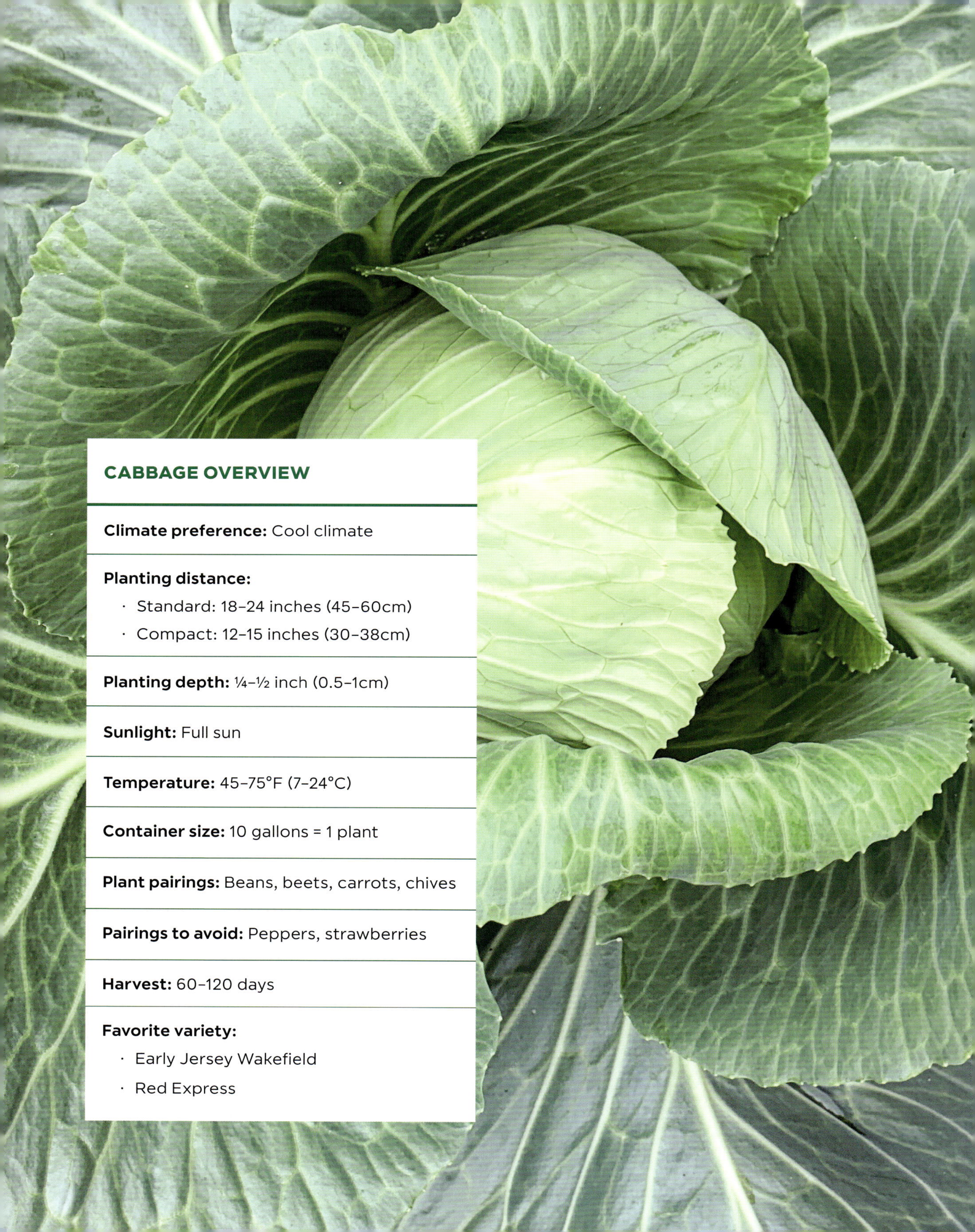

CABBAGE OVERVIEW

Climate preference: Cool climate

Planting distance:
- Standard: 18–24 inches (45–60cm)
- Compact: 12–15 inches (30–38cm)

Planting depth: ¼–½ inch (0.5–1cm)

Sunlight: Full sun

Temperature: 45–75°F (7–24°C)

Container size: 10 gallons = 1 plant

Plant pairings: Beans, beets, carrots, chives

Pairings to avoid: Peppers, strawberries

Harvest: 60–120 days

Favorite variety:
- Early Jersey Wakefield
- Red Express

CABBAGE

Growing cabbage was a challenge for us, as they often split. After experimenting with many varieties, we landed on Early Jersey Wakefield, which thrives in our region due to their shorter growing season, so we finally enjoyed a successful harvest. Persistence truly pays off in the garden!

Planting Cabbage 101

In cool climates, you should start your cabbage seeds indoors about 6 to 8 weeks before the last frost date. When seedlings have 4 to 5 true leaves and outdoor temperatures are consistently above 45°F (7°C), they can be transplanted into the garden, usually 2 to 3 weeks before the last spring frost. In temperate climates, you can plant cabbage seeds directly in the ground about 4 to 6 weeks before the last expected frost. Plant seeds ¼ to ½ inch (0.5 to 1cm) deep, water gently, and keep the soil consistently moist. When transplanting, space the cabbage plants 18 to 24 inches (45 to 60cm) apart for standard spacing, or 12 to 15 inches (30 to 38cm) apart for a compact garden.

Growing Cabbage 101

Water your cabbage plants 2 to 3 times per week, adjusting based on your climate. After transplanting at 2 to 3 weeks, enrich the soil with compost or aged manure, then feed the plants with a high-nitrogen amendment like fish emulsion or blood meal every 2 to 3 weeks.

Growing Cabbage in Pots

The ideal container size for one cabbage plant is at least 10 to 15 gallons, and 12 inches (30cm) deep and 18 inches (45cm) wide. Use potting mix with compost for added nutrients, and place the pot where it can receive 6 to 8 hours of sunlight a day.

Optional Amendments

- **Compost:** Mix into the soil before planting, and optionally top dress halfway through the growing season.
- **Blood meal:** Side dress with blood meal, particularly during the early stages of growth.
- **Liquid seaweed or fish emulsion:** Apply every 2 to 3 weeks.

Challenges

Common pests include cabbage worms, leaf miners, aphids, and flea beetles. Use lightweight row covers, especially for young plants, and inspect regularly and handpick pests. These plants are prone to black rot and downy mildew in wet conditions, so avoid overhead watering, and rotate crops yearly. Cabbage heads can split from rapid growth or uneven watering—water consistently, and harvest when heads are firm and mature.

CARROTS

We used to grow weird-looking carrots, but even though they looked odd, they tasted amazing! After we improved our soil and planted carrots at the right time, we started pulling up nice, straight carrots. The best part was that we got bonus carrots by planting them next to our pepper plants, which proved to us that growing different plants together helps us use our small space better and gives us higher yields.

Planting Carrots 101

Carrots grow best in cool weather. In most areas, you should plant seeds in early spring, as soon as the soil can be worked, or in late summer for a fall harvest, 3 to 4 weeks before the last frost. It's best to plant the seeds directly in the ground. Choose a sunny spot and loosen the soil to make it fluffy and crumbly. We add a layer of compost about 1 inch (0.5cm) thick but avoid using aged manure, as it can be too rich for young carrots. Standard spacing is 2 to 3 inches (5 to 7.5cm) apart, with compact spacing at 1 to 2 inches (2.5 to 5cm) apart. Since carrot seeds are tiny and delicate, be gentle when sowing at ¼ inch (0.5cm) deep and lightly cover them with soil.

Growing Carrots 101

Water lightly but often to keep the soil moist. Carrots thrive in nutrient-rich soil, so it's a good idea to mix in compost before planting. During the growing season, feed with compost every 4 to 6 weeks. Avoid fertilizers high in nitrogen, as they lead to leafy tops but small roots. Instead, use balanced amendments with phosphorus and potassium, like bone meal and kelp meal, to help the roots develop.

Growing Carrots in Pots

Choose a container at least 12 inches (30cm) deep for standard carrots, or 6 to 8 inches (15 to 20cm) for dwarf carrots. Use a well-draining potting mix that's loose to encourage straight growth, and mix in compost and a handful of bone meal for root development. Sow seeds with plants like peppers for an extra abundant harvest.

Optional Amendments

- **Compost:** Add a layer before planting, and a fresh thin layer every 4 to 6 weeks.
- **Bone meal:** Add before planting, or lightly around the plants during the growing season.
- **Worm castings:** Add midseason.

Challenges

One common problem is uneven germination, which happens if the soil dries out before the seeds sprout. To prevent this, keep the soil consistently moist during the first few weeks. Another issue is forked or twisted carrots, which usually occurs when the soil is rocky or compacted. Always loosen the soil before planting to avoid this, or choose a variety that features short, conical roots, like Danvers. Pests like carrot flies can damage your crop by laying eggs near the plants, and their larvae feed on the roots. Cover the carrot bed with fine mesh, or grow carrots alongside strong-smelling plants like onions or garlic, which help repel pests.

CARROTS OVERVIEW

Climate preference: Cool climate

Planting distance:
- Standard: 2–3 inches (5–7.5cm)
- Compact: 1–2 inches (2.5–5cm)

Planting depth: ¼ inch (0.5cm)

Sunlight: Full sun, light shade

Temperature: 55–75°F (13–24°C)

Container size: 5 gallons = 8 to 10 plants

Plant pairings: Onions, leeks, radishes, peppers

Pairings to avoid: Dill, parsnips, fennel

Harvest: 60–80 days

Favorite variety:
- Purple Dragon
- Rainbow Mix

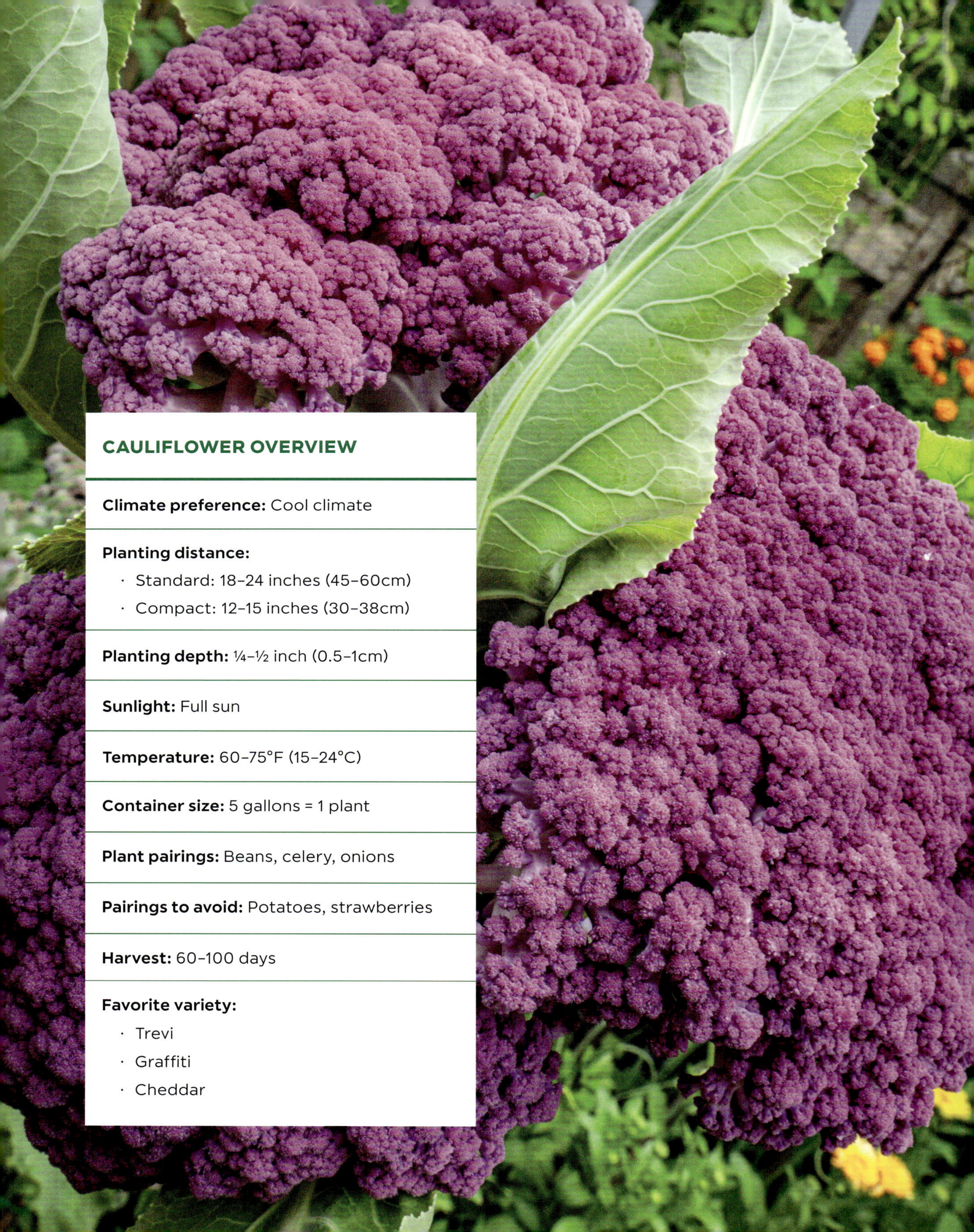

CAULIFLOWER OVERVIEW

Climate preference: Cool climate

Planting distance:
- Standard: 18–24 inches (45–60cm)
- Compact: 12–15 inches (30–38cm)

Planting depth: ¼–½ inch (0.5–1cm)

Sunlight: Full sun

Temperature: 60–75°F (15–24°C)

Container size: 5 gallons = 1 plant

Plant pairings: Beans, celery, onions

Pairings to avoid: Potatoes, strawberries

Harvest: 60–100 days

Favorite variety:
- Trevi
- Graffiti
- Cheddar

CAULIFLOWER

When we thought of cauliflower, it was a plain white vegetable in our minds. But then we stumbled upon the colorful cauliflower revolution! Suddenly, we were introduced to Trevi, a stunning green variety; Graffiti, the purple beauty; and Cheddar, the orange variety that practically begs to be in your mac and cheese.

Planting Cauliflower 101

Cauliflower thrives in mild temperatures, ideally between 60 to 75°F (15 to 24°C). You can plant in early spring for a summer harvest or in late summer for a fall harvest. When planting directly in the ground, make sure the soil temperature is at least 50°F (10°C) for seeds to germinate. Adding aged manure or compost helps the soil. In cool climates, it's best to start seeds indoors 6 to 8 weeks before the last frost. You can also sow seeds directly 2 to 3 weeks before the last frost, planting them ¼ to ½ inch (0.5 to 1cm) deep, or transplant seedlings 4 to 6 weeks before the last frost, ideally under cover. Standard spacing is 18 to 24 inches (45 to 60cm) apart, but you can plant them 12 to 15 inches (30 to 38cm) apart to save space.

Growing Cauliflower 101

Cauliflower prefers moist soil, so be sure to water it 2 to 3 times per week, keeping the soil evenly moist. For optimal growth, cauliflower needs loose, fertile soil that drains well. As the cauliflower heads develop, you can use a technique called blanching, which entails tying the outer leaves over the head to protect it from sunlight and help it stay white and tender. However, this step isn't necessary for self-blanching or colored varieties. Use row covers to keep the plants safe from frost, hot weather, and pests. To feed your cauliflower, start with nitrogen, like aged manure or fish emulsion, every 2 to 4 weeks to help the leaves grow. Once the heads start to form, switch to a phosphorus-rich fertilizer, like bone meal, to help the curds develop. Adding lime to the soil is believed to enhance sweetness.

Growing Cauliflower in Pots

Choose a container that holds at least 5 gallons, and is 12 to 18 inches (30 to 45cm) deep for adequate root space. Fertilize every 2 to 3 weeks with organic liquid fertilizer, like fish emulsion.

Optional Amendments

- **Compost:** Apply once during soil preparation.
- **Bone meal:** Add when transplanting and once more midseason.
- **Fish emulsion:** Feed during the early stages every 2 to 4 weeks, and stop when the heads start to form.

Challenges

Watch out for aphids, cabbage worms, and flea beetles, which damage leaves and heads. To control aphids, plant trap crops like nasturtium, or use beneficial insects like ladybugs. Cauliflower heads can become button-like due to inconsistent watering, temperature changes, or nutrient deficiencies. Provide consistent watering and use a balanced fertilizer regularly. Cauliflower can get black rot and powdery mildew in humid conditions, so ensure good airflow, avoid overhead watering, and practice crop rotation.

CELERY

When we first grew celery, we started from kitchen scraps. We took the base of a store-bought celery and placed it in a bowl of water, and new shoots grew from the center. After a few weeks, we planted those scraps in the garden, and they turned into delicious celery.

Planting Celery 101

Plant celery in early spring or late summer. In warm climates, it can grow through the cooler months. When planting seeds directly in the ground, wait until the soil is at least 50°F (10°C). Sow seeds ¼ inch (0.5cm) deep, or scatter seeds on the soil, lightly cover them, and keep the soil moist. In cool climates, start seeds indoors 10 to 12 weeks before the last frost to give them time to germinate. We use a 3-inch (7.5cm) pot, sprinkle seeds on top, cover lightly, and water gently. Keep pots under grow lights. Once the seedlings are 4 to 6 inches (10 to 15cm) tall with 2 to 3 true leaves, move them outside when it's frost free. Transplant seedlings when the outdoor soil temperature stays above 50°F (10°C), and be sure to harden off seedlings outdoors for a week before planting. Standard spacing is 8 to 12 inches (20 to 30cm) apart, or 6 to 8 inches (15 to 20cm) apart for tighter planting. Closer spacing may result in smaller stalks. Add aged manure or compost to the soil before transplanting, and water well.

Growing Celery 101

Celery thrives in consistently moist soil, so aim to water 3 to 4 times per week, depending on the weather. Use row covers for the first few weeks to control pests. Celery is a heavy feeder and needs rich soil, so add compost or a liquid seaweed fertilizer every 2 to 3 weeks.

Growing Celery in Pots

Celery can thrive in containers if you choose the right size. The ideal container should be at least 5 gallons and about 12 inches (30cm) deep to accommodate the root system. You can grow one celery plant per container or plant multiple stalks in a large pot, spacing them about 6 to 8 inches (15 to 20cm) apart. Use potting mix with compost and water deeply.

Optional Amendments

- **Compost:** Add a layer before planting.
- **Aged manure:** Apply around the plants about 4 weeks after transplanting.
- **Liquid seaweed fertilizer:** Use a diluted liquid seaweed fertilizer every 2 to 3 weeks.

Challenges

If the weather gets too hot or if the plants are stressed, celery may bolt and produce flowers instead of stalks. To prevent this, plant celery at the right time and keep the soil consistently moist. Watch out for aphids, slugs, and celery leaf miners. You can handpick pests, use natural insecticidal sprays, or introduce beneficial insects like ladybugs. Yellow leaves are often a sign of nutrient deficiency. Add compost or a liquid seaweed fertilizer to correct the issue

CELERY OVERVIEW

Climate preference: Cool climate

Planting distance:
- Standard: 8–12 inches (20–30cm)
- Compact: 6–8 inches (15–20cm)

Planting depth: ¼ inch (0.5cm)

Sunlight: Full sun

Temperature: 60–75°F (15–24°C)

Container size: 10 gallons = 2 to 3 plants

Plant pairings: Beans, brassicas, spinach

Pairings to avoid: Potatoes, carrots, parsnips

Harvest: 80–120 days

Favorite variety:
- Tall Utah
- Golden Self Blanching

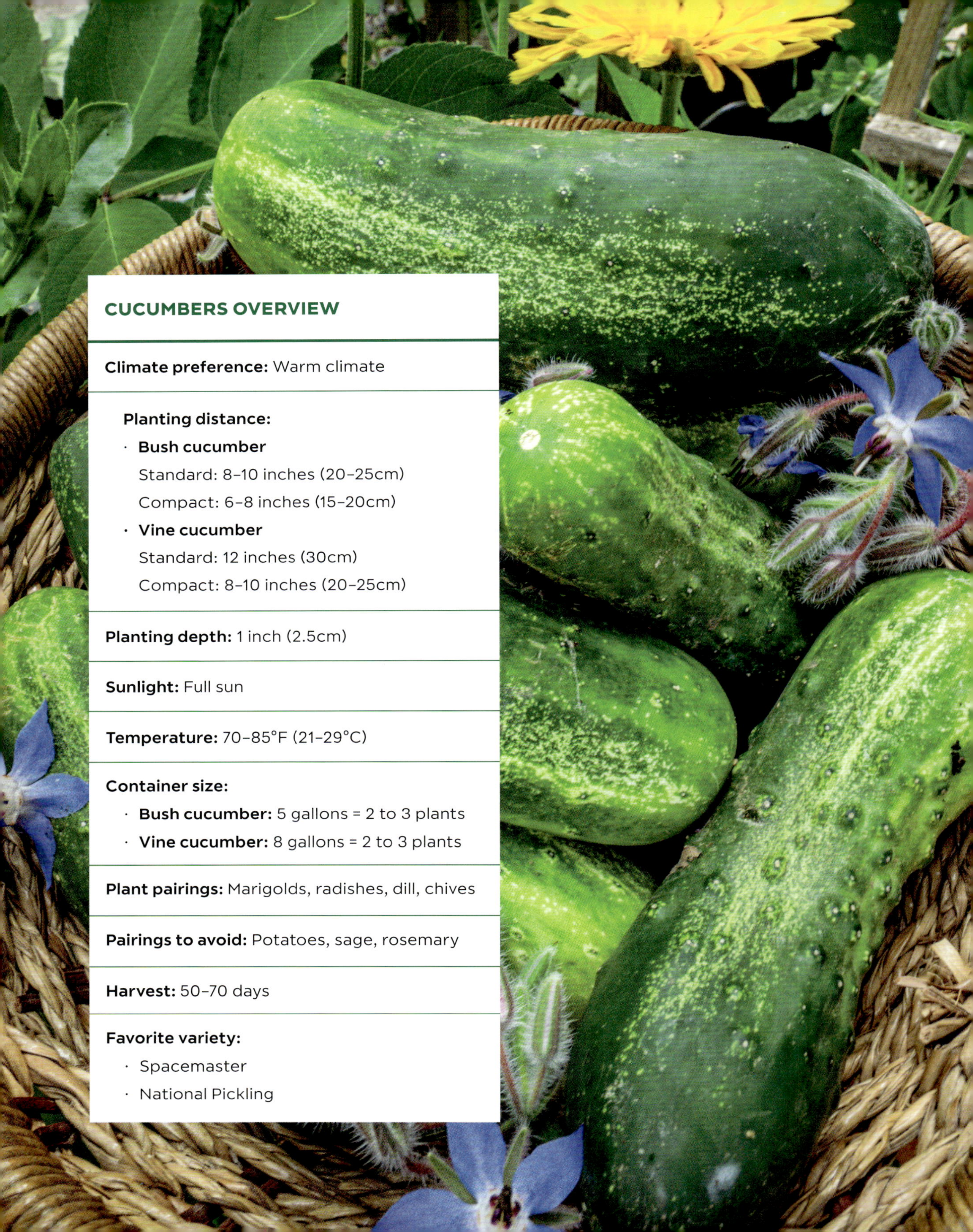

CUCUMBERS OVERVIEW

Climate preference: Warm climate

Planting distance:
· Bush cucumber
Standard: 8–10 inches (20–25cm)
Compact: 6–8 inches (15–20cm)
· Vine cucumber
Standard: 12 inches (30cm)
Compact: 8–10 inches (20–25cm)

Planting depth: 1 inch (2.5cm)

Sunlight: Full sun

Temperature: 70–85°F (21–29°C)

Container size:
· Bush cucumber: 5 gallons = 2 to 3 plants
· Vine cucumber: 8 gallons = 2 to 3 plants

Plant pairings: Marigolds, radishes, dill, chives

Pairings to avoid: Potatoes, sage, rosemary

Harvest: 50–70 days

Favorite variety:
· Spacemaster
· National Pickling

CUCUMBERS

There are two main growth types of cucumbers. Bush cucumbers are compact plants that grow in a mounded shape and don't need support, making them ideal for small gardens and containers. Vining cucumbers are climbing varieties that grow long, trailing vines and need trellises or other supports but typically produce higher yields. For vining cucumbers, be sure to leave room on the ground for companion plants like marigolds or basil.

Planting Cucumbers 101

The best time to plant seeds directly in the ground is after the last frost and when the soil is around 70°F (21°C). Prepare the soil by adding compost or aged manure. Sow seeds 1 inch (2.5cm) deep, cover with soil, and water gently. For vining types, standard spacing is 12 inches (30cm) apart, and compact spacing is 8 to 10 inches (20 to 25cm) apart if using a trellis. Bush varieties are smaller, so standard spacing is 8 to 10 inches (20 to 25cm) apart, and compact spacing is 6 to 8 inches (15 to 20cm) apart. In cool climates, start cucumber seeds indoors 3 to 4 weeks before the last frost. Plant seeds 1 inch (2.5cm) deep in pots, and keep them warm and under grow lights. Once seedlings have 2 true leaves and the outdoor soil is warm enough, harden them off for 7 to 10 days before planting them.

Growing Cucumbers 101

Cucumbers need a lot of water, so keep the nitrogen-rich soil moist. Add compost or aged manure into the soil when you plant them. After they start to flower, feed them every 3 to 4 weeks with bone meal. Some cucumber plants sprawl, so use a trellis to support them. To help cucumbers produce fruit, you can hand-pollinate: Use a small brush or your finger to move pollen from the male flowers (which have thin stems) to the female flowers (which have a tiny fruit at the base).

Growing Cucumbers in Pots

Choose a large container with good drainage—ideally at least 5 to 8 gallons, and 12 inches (30cm) wide and 12 to 18 inches (30 to 45cm) deep. A trellis or stake helps to support climbing varieties. Use a potting mix enriched with compost. Sow 4 to 5 seeds per container, and thin them out to the strongest seedling once they've sprouted. Water deeply and fertilize every 2 to 3 weeks.

Optional Amendments

· **Compost:** Mix into the soil before planting, and top dress around the plants every 4 to 6 weeks.
· **Comfrey or nettle tea:** Apply every 1 to 2 weeks during the flowering or fruiting stage, as it's high in potassium.
· **Bone meal:** Apply every 3 to 4 weeks for added phosphorus nutrients.

Challenges

Common pests are aphids, cucumber beetles, and spider mites. Cucumber beetles can cause damage to leaves and flowers and may spread bacterial wilt and mosaic virus, which can destroy plants. Control pests early using row covers, companion planting with chives or marigolds, organic insecticides like kaolin clay, or handpicking.

EGGPLANT

In our cool climate, we've found that eggplants grow much better in containers than in the ground. Containers help the soil warm up faster because they're above ground level and exposed to air circulation on all sides, plus their walls absorb and retain heat from the sun throughout the day, which is great because eggplants love heat. Plus, it's easier to take care of the soil, water them, and keep pests away, meaning healthier plants and more delicious eggplants to enjoy.

Planting Eggplant 101

Choose a location that gets at least 6 to 8 hours of full sun. Eggplants can also tolerate partial shade. If planting seeds directly into the ground, wait until the soil is consistently warm, around 70°F (21°C), since eggplant seeds won't germinate well in cool soil. When planting, standard spacing is 24 to 36 inches (60 to 90cm) apart for full-size eggplants. However, we plant them closer, at 8 to 10 inches (20 to 25cm) apart; just be sure to give them extra care if you do the same. In cool climates, start seeds indoors 8 to 10 weeks before your last frost date. Sow seeds ¼ inch (0.5cm) deep. Keep the soil moist and warm, ideally between 75 and 85°F (24 to 29°C), to encourage germination. Use a heating mat, and place under grow lights. Once the seedlings are 3 to 4 inches (7.5 to 10cm) tall and have at least 2 sets of true leaves, they're ready to transplant outdoors. Harden off about a week before planting them in the garden.

Growing Eggplant 101

Water deeply and amend the soil with compost or aged manure at planting, and again every 4 to 6 weeks through the growing season. We like to add bone meal once they start flowering. Additionally, staking can help support heavy fruit and prevent the branches from breaking.

Growing Eggplant in Pots

Choose a container that holds at least 5 gallons (larger is even better) to give the roots plenty of room to grow. It should be 8 to 12 inches (20 to 30cm) deep. Keep the container in a sunny spot, water deeply, and feed every 2 to 3 weeks with compost or fish emulsion.

Optional Amendments

- **Compost:** Add in at planting and as a top dressing every 4 to 6 weeks.
- **Bone meal:** Add to the soil when planting and once more when the plants start flowering.
- **Fish emulsion:** Use every 2 to 3 weeks.

Challenges

Common pests are aphids, flea beetles, and spider mites, which can damage the leaves and make the plant less productive. Use homemade insecticidal soap, or plant marigolds, basil, or nasturtiums nearby. Blight and wilt occur in humid weather—prevent this by avoiding overwatering, ensuring airflow, and rotating crops yearly. Flowers falling off without fruit is due to heat or stress. Ensure adequate watering and protect from temperature changes.

EGGPLANT OVERVIEW

Climate preference: Warm climate

Planting distance:
- Standard: 24–36 inches (60–90cm)
- Compact: 8–10 inches (20–25cm)

Planting depth: ¼ inch (0.5cm)

Sunlight: Full sun, partial shade

Temperature: 70–85°F (21–29°C)

Container size: 10 gallons = 2 to 3 plants

Plant pairings: Beans, basil, peppers

Pairings to avoid: Potatoes, corn, fennel

Harvest: 60–80 days

Favorite variety:
- Fingerling
- Black Beauty

GARLIC OVERVIEW

Climate preference: Cool climate

Planting distance: 4–6 inches (10–15cm)

Planting depth: 2–4 inches (5–10cm)

Sunlight: Full sun

Temperature: 55–75°F (13–24°C)

Container size: 5 gallons = 3 to 4 plants

Plant pairings: Carrots, beets, spinach

Pairings to avoid: Peas, beans, sage

Harvest: 210–270 days

Favorite variety:
· Music
· Red Russian

GARLIC

There are two main types of garlic: hardneck and softneck. Hardneck garlic has a stiff stalk and grows fewer but larger bulbs, doing well in cooler climates. Softneck garlic has a flexible stalk, produces more cloves that are smaller, and thrives in warmer climates—this variety is what you usually find in stores.

Planting Garlic 101

Garlic needs a cold period of 32 to 50°F (0 to 10°C), called vernalization, to help the cloves turn into bulbs. In warm areas, this means keeping them in the fridge until planting. In our cool climate, we plant hardneck garlic in the fall, 4 to 6 weeks before the ground freezes. Choose a spot that gets 6 to 8 hours of full sunlight, and add a layer of compost about an inch thick. To plant, break apart a garlic bulb and select the biggest cloves, keeping the smaller ones for cooking. For spacing, if you want bigger bulbs, plant the cloves 6 inches (15cm) apart. If your soil is loose, plant the cloves 4 inches (10cm) deep. In harder soil, plant them 2 inches (5cm) deep, measuring from the pointy tip of the garlic to the soil surface. After planting, lightly cover them with soil and add a layer of 4 to 6 inches (10 to 15cm) of brown leaves. This acts as extra protection for your garlic once the ground starts to freeze.

Growing Garlic 101

Feed your garlic with a good compost in the spring when the sprouts appear. You can then apply a nitrogen-rich amendment like blood meal every 3 to 4 weeks during the growing season, until the bulbs start to form. It's important to water regularly, at least 2 to 3 times per week. When growing hardneck garlic, it will start to produce a flowering stem known as garlic scape. This part is edible and should be removed when it reaches a full curl. By removing the scape, the plant's energy will be redirected to producing bigger bulbs. Garlic can be harvested around July and August. It's important to stop watering your garlic 2 to 3 weeks before harvesting to allow the soil to dry out, encouraging the outer layers of the garlic bulbs to harden and form a protective skin. This skin is essential for long-term storage.

Growing Garlic in Pots

Garlic is best planted directly in the ground or in garden beds, but it can also be done in containers. If you're growing on a balcony, for example, a 5-gallon container is sufficient to grow at least 3 to 4 garlic cloves.

Optional Amendments

- **Compost:** Add into the soil before planting.
- **Blood meal:** Sprinkle a small amount around the garlic plants 2 to 4 weeks after planting.
- **Bone meal:** Mix into the planting hole when you place each garlic clove into the soil.
- **Chicken-manure granules:** Feed every 4 to 6 weeks.

Challenges

Onion maggots and thrips can damage garlic plants. Use row covers to protect your crop or plant alongside pest-repelling companions like marigold and chives.

LETTUCE

Lettuce is like the gardener's best friend: It's easygoing, quick to sprout, and versatile enough to grow almost anywhere.

Planting Lettuce 101

In early spring, sow seeds 2 to 4 weeks before the last frost. If you have a cold frame, you can plant 4 to 6 weeks before the last frost. For a fall harvest, plant 6 to 8 weeks before the first frost. Choose cold-tolerant types of lettuce for growing in the spring and fall, and heat-tolerant ones for the summer. We like to keep it simple and sow seeds outdoors 3 to 4 weeks before the last frost, planting them about ¼ inch (0.5cm) deep and 6 to 8 inches (15 to 20cm) apart. If space is tight, you can plant them closer, although that may lead to smaller heads. In our garden, we plant seeds 1 to 2 inches (2.5 to 5cm) apart for baby leaves, then thin them out by removing every other one. Cover the seeds lightly with soil, water gently, and let nature do its thing!

Growing Lettuce 101

Water 2 to 3 times per week, depending on your climate. To keep your lettuce happy and thriving, feed it with organic matter. Lettuce is a light feeder, so it doesn't require tons of fertilizer, but it does appreciate rich, well-amended soil. Add a layer of compost or aged manure to the soil before planting and side dress your plants with more compost about once a month during the growing season.

Growing Lettuce in Pots

The ideal container size depends on how many plants you want to grow, but a 2- to 3-gallon container is perfect for 2 to 3 heads of lettuce. Just make sure the container is at least 6 inches (15cm) deep.

Optional Amendments

- **Compost:** Add a layer before planting and refresh every 4 weeks.
- **Worm castings:** Mix into the soil or use as a top dressing every 6 weeks.
- **Fish emulsion:** Dilute with water and apply every 3 to 4 weeks.

Challenges

Slugs and snails love nibbling on tender lettuce leaves; handpicking them is your best bet. You can also plant chives or cilantro to detract pests with their strong smell.

LETTUCE OVERVIEW

Climate preference: Cold climate

Planting distance:
· Standard: 6–8 inches (15–20cm)
· Compact: 4–6 inches (10–15cm)

Planting depth: ¼ inch (0.5cm)

Sunlight: Full sun, partial shade

Temperature: 60–70°F (15–21°C)

Container size: 1 gallon = 1 plant

Plant pairings: Carrots, radishes

Pairings to avoid: Celery, cabbages

Harvest: 30–70 days

Favorite variety:
· Parris Island Cos
· Red Sails

ONIONS OVERVIEW

Climate preference: Cool climate

Planting distance:
· Standard: 6 inches (15cm)
· Compact: 3 inches (7.5cm)

Planting depth:
· Seeds: ¼ inch (0.5cm)
· Sets: 1 inch (2.5cm)

Sunlight: Full sun

Temperature: 55–75°F (13–24°C)

Container size: 5 gallons = 3 to 4 plants

Plant pairings: Carrots, lettuce, beets

Pairings to avoid: Peas, beans, asparagus

Harvest: 100–120 days

Favorite variety:
· Yellow Sweet Spanish
· Walla Walla

ONIONS

We initially struggled because we didn't realize there are three types of onions: short day, intermediate, and long day. Short-day onions thrive in warmer climates with shorter daylight hours (10 to 12 hours). Long-day onions, as the name suggests, need longer days (14 to 16 hours), making them ideal for northern regions, especially during the summer solstice. Intermediate onions fall in between, growing well in areas with a mix of daylight lengths (12 to 14 hours). Once we learned that long-day onions were best for us, our results improved.

Planting Onions 101

Onions can be grown from sets (small bulbs), seedlings, or seeds. To plant sets, place them about 1 inch (2.5cm) deep and 6 inches (15cm) apart in well-draining soil with compost and full sun. We prefer starting from seeds because it lets us choose from many varieties. If planting seeds directly, wait until the soil reaches at least 50°F (10°C). For full-size bulbs, sow seeds ¼ inch (0.5cm) deep and space them 6 inches (15cm) apart. In smaller spaces, you can plant them 3 inches (7.5cm) apart, but the bulbs may be smaller. In cool climates, start seeds indoors 8 to 10 weeks before the last frost. Once seedlings are 6 inches (15cm) tall with 3 leaves, trim them to 4 inches (10cm) and feed them fish emulsion every 2 weeks. This helps them grow healthy roots and thicker stems. Transplant seedlings into the garden 2 to 4 weeks before the last frost for the best results.

Growing Onions 101

Onions have shallow root systems and like their soil to be moist but not too wet. They are heavy feeders, so in the early stages, use a nitrogen amendment like blood meal every few weeks to help them grow. Once the onions start to push up from the soil and form bulbs later in the season, switch to bone meal to help their roots and bulbs grow. When the leaves start turning yellow, stop feeding them, because they're almost ready to harvest.

Growing Onions in Pots

A container that holds at least 5 gallons with 10 inches (25cm) of depth works well for growing onions and can accommodate 3 to 4 plants. Space seeds or sets about 3 inches (7.5cm) apart and place the container where it'll receive 6 to 8 hours of direct sunlight daily.

Optional Amendments

- **Compost:** Mix in before planting and top dress every few weeks.
- **Bone meal:** Apply at planting time and again midseason.
- **Seaweed liquid fertilizer:** Use every 2 to 3 weeks.

Challenges

Pests like onion maggots and thrips can damage your plants. Practice crop rotation and use floating row covers for protection. To prevent onions from bolting, ensure they're planted at the right time for your climate, provide consistent moisture, and avoid exposing them to extreme temperature changes.

PEAS

Peas are the perfect crop for a compact garden because they grow tall, so you can save space while still getting a delicious harvest. There are three types of peas to pick from: garden peas, which are sweet and juicy seeds found inside pods; snow peas, which have flat, tender pods; and snap peas, which are crunchy and sweet and whose whole pod is entirely edible. Peas do best when you plant the seeds directly in the ground because they sprout so easily.

Planting Peas 101

Peas thrive in cool weather, making them one of the first crops you can plant in the spring. The soil should be at least 40°F (4°C) because peas grow best in cool but not freezing weather. If the soil is too wet, the seeds can rot, so it's important to have good drainage. Peas grow most optimally in full sun, ideally 6 to 8 hours of sunlight daily, but can tolerate partial shade. To plant peas, sow the seeds directly into the ground. Dig a shallow trench about 1 inch (2.5cm) deep, place the seeds in the trench, and cover them lightly with soil. Standard spacing is 2 to 3 inches (5 to 7.5cm) apart, but if you're working with a compact garden and want to maximize space, you can plant them 1 inch (2.5cm) apart. Just keep in mind that closer spacing might require a little extra care to ensure good airflow.

Growing Peas 101

Peas like consistent moisture, so water regularly. They don't need to be fed, but adding compost before planting can help them grow better. Peas are climbing plants, so install a trellis, stakes, or twine to help them climb upward.

Growing Peas in Pots

Pick a container that's at least 5 gallons to fit 6 to 8 pea plants, and make sure it's at least 8 inches (20cm) deep with good drainage holes. Remember to provide support when they start to climb.

Optional Amendments

· **Compost:** Mix into the soil before planting.

Challenges

Common pests include aphids, weevils, and slugs. To control aphids, spray the plants with a strong jet of water, and handpick slugs and weevils. You can plant marigolds or borage nearby to pull pests away and bring in beneficial bugs.

PEAS OVERVIEW

Climate preference: Cool climate

Planting distance:
- Standard: 2–3 inches (5–7.5cm)
- Compact: 1 inch (2.5cm)

Planting depth: 1 inch (2.5cm)

Sunlight: Full sun, partial shade

Temperature: 40–70°F (4–21°C)

Container size: 5 gallons = 6 to 8 plants

Plant pairings: Carrots, lettuce, radishes

Pairings to avoid: Garlic, onions, leeks

Harvest: 60–70 days

Favorite variety:
- Sugar Ann
- Oregon Sugar Pod II

PEPPERS OVERVIEW

Climate preference: Warm climate

Planting distance:
· Standard: 18–24 inches (45–60cm)
· Compact: 12 inches (30cm)

Planting depth: ¼ inch (0.5cm)

Sunlight: Full sun

Temperature: 70–85°F (21–29°C)

Container size: 5 gallons = 1 plant

Plant pairings: Carrots, onions, tomatoes

Pairings to avoid: Fennel, brassicas, beans

Harvest: 60–90 days

Favorite variety:
· Siling labuyo
· Wiri Wiri

PEPPERS

At first, our pepper harvests were small because of the short growing season in Canada. Eventually, we learned that if we planted the seeds in early January, they would have enough time to grow and give us three harvests in our three-month season.

Planting Peppers 101

If you live in a warm climate, you can plant pepper seeds directly in the ground when the soil is at least 65°F (18°C). Standard spacing is 18 to 24 inches (45 to 60cm) apart or 12 inches (30cm) apart for a smaller garden. In cool climates, it's best to start seeds indoors around January to help them grow strong. Use small trays with a seed-starting mix, planting seeds ¼ inch (0.5cm) deep. Keep the soil moist, place under grow lights, and use a humidity dome in a warm spot set between 70 and 85°F (21 and 29°C). Peppers can take 7 to 21 days to sprout, so be patient. Once the seeds start to grow, take off the dome cover. When the seedlings have 4 true leaves, move them to bigger containers. Remove any early flowers so the plants can focus on growing. When outdoor temperatures are consistently above 50°F (10°C) at night, it's time to harden them off outdoors over 7 to 10 days. Once hardened, they're ready for transplant. Choose a location that gets 6 to 8 hours of full sun. Before planting, add chicken-manure granules, gypsum, and rock dust to the soil.

Growing Peppers 101

Watering peppers is all about balance. They like soil that is consistently moist but not soaking wet. Water deeply 2 to 3 times per week, depending on your climate. To ensure your peppers thrive, feed them monthly with a handful of chicken-manure granules around the base of each plant, then mix into the soil and water well. As the plants grow, you may notice they'll need some support. If they're loaded with peppers, use stakes to keep the stems from breaking.

Growing Peppers in Pots

The key is to choose a container big enough for the plant to grow and thrive. Ideally, use a 5-gallon container with at least 12 inches (30cm) of depth per plant. Make sure the container has good drainage holes. Use a potting mix and add in natural amendments like chicken-manure granules, gypsum, and rock dust before planting. Place the container in a sunny spot that gets at least 6 hours of sunlight per day. Container peppers need more frequent watering than those in the ground.

Optional Amendments

· **Gypsum:** Add to the soil once when planting your peppers.
· **Chicken-manure granules:** Apply a handful every month.
· **Rock dust:** Add before planting and a little midseason.

Challenges

Aphids, spider mites, and slugs are frequent visitors to pepper plants. You can introduce natural predators like ladybugs to help control aphids. To combat slugs, handpicking is often the easiest solution. You can also grow marigolds, calendula, or nasturtiums beside your peppers to help deter pests and attract beneficial bugs.

POTATOES

Nothing beats freshly dug potatoes, and growing them yourself means they're free from harmful chemicals. We've successfully regrown organic potatoes from the grocery store, but it's best to use certified seed potatoes because they are free of diseases. Purchase once and save some from your harvest to replant year after year for an endless supply.

Planting Potatoes 101
Potatoes grow best in cooler weather, so they should be planted in the spring or fall. In cool climates, the ideal time to plant is 2 to 4 weeks before the last frost in spring. The soil should be cool, around 50°F (10°C), and not too wet, as soggy soil can make seed potatoes rot. Use potatoes with at least 1 to 2 eyes (the dimples where sprouts grow). If they're large, you can cut them into smaller pieces, ensuring each piece has eyes. Let them sit for 1 to 2 days. To plant, dig trenches about 4 to 6 inches (10 to 15cm) deep. Standard spacing is 12 inches (30cm) apart or 6 inches (15cm) apart in a compact space, though this may yield smaller potatoes. Cover them with loose soil and water lightly.

Growing Potatoes 101
As the plants grow, you'll need to hill them, which means mounding soil around the base of the plants to prevent sunlight from reaching the potatoes. Hill your potatoes every couple of weeks or whenever you see new growth emerging from the soil. Potato plants need consistent watering, especially during the flowering stage when tubers are forming. Aim to water deeply 2 to 3 times per week, ensuring the soil stays moist. Potatoes are heavy feeders and benefit from natural amendments like compost or bone meal. Apply a layer of compost when planting, and add another layer midseason when hilling the potatoes.

Growing Potatoes in Pots
Choose a container that's at least 15 gallons for 2 to 3 seed potatoes. Fill the bottom of the container with 4 to 6 inches (10 to 15cm) of potting soil mixed with compost. Place the seed potatoes on top, and cover them with another 4 inches (10cm) of soil. As the plants grow, continue adding soil to keep the developing tubers covered. Be sure the container has drainage holes to prevent water from pooling at the bottom, and water to keep the soil evenly moist.

Optional Amendments
- **Compost:** Apply when planting and again midseason when hilling your potatoes.
- **Bone meal:** Mix into the soil at planting time.
- **Kelp meal:** Use every 4 to 6 weeks during the growing season.

Challenges
The Colorado potato beetle is a striped bug that eats potato leaves quickly—it's best to use row covers to keep them away or handpick off plants when you notice them. Companion-plant chives, onions, or garlic to help keep pests away, and plant flowering cilantro nearby, as it attracts helpful insects like hoverflies and ladybugs.

POTATOES OVERVIEW

Climate preference: Cool climate

Planting distance:
Standard: 12 inches (30cm)
Compact: 6 inches (15cm)

Planting depth: 4–6 inches (10–15cm)

Sunlight: Full sun

Temperature: 50–70°F (10–21°C)

Container size: 15 gallons = 2 to 3 plants

Plant pairings: Beans, celery, corn

Pairings to avoid: Carrots, parsnips

Harvest: 90–120 days

Favorite variety:
Yukon Gold
Chieftain

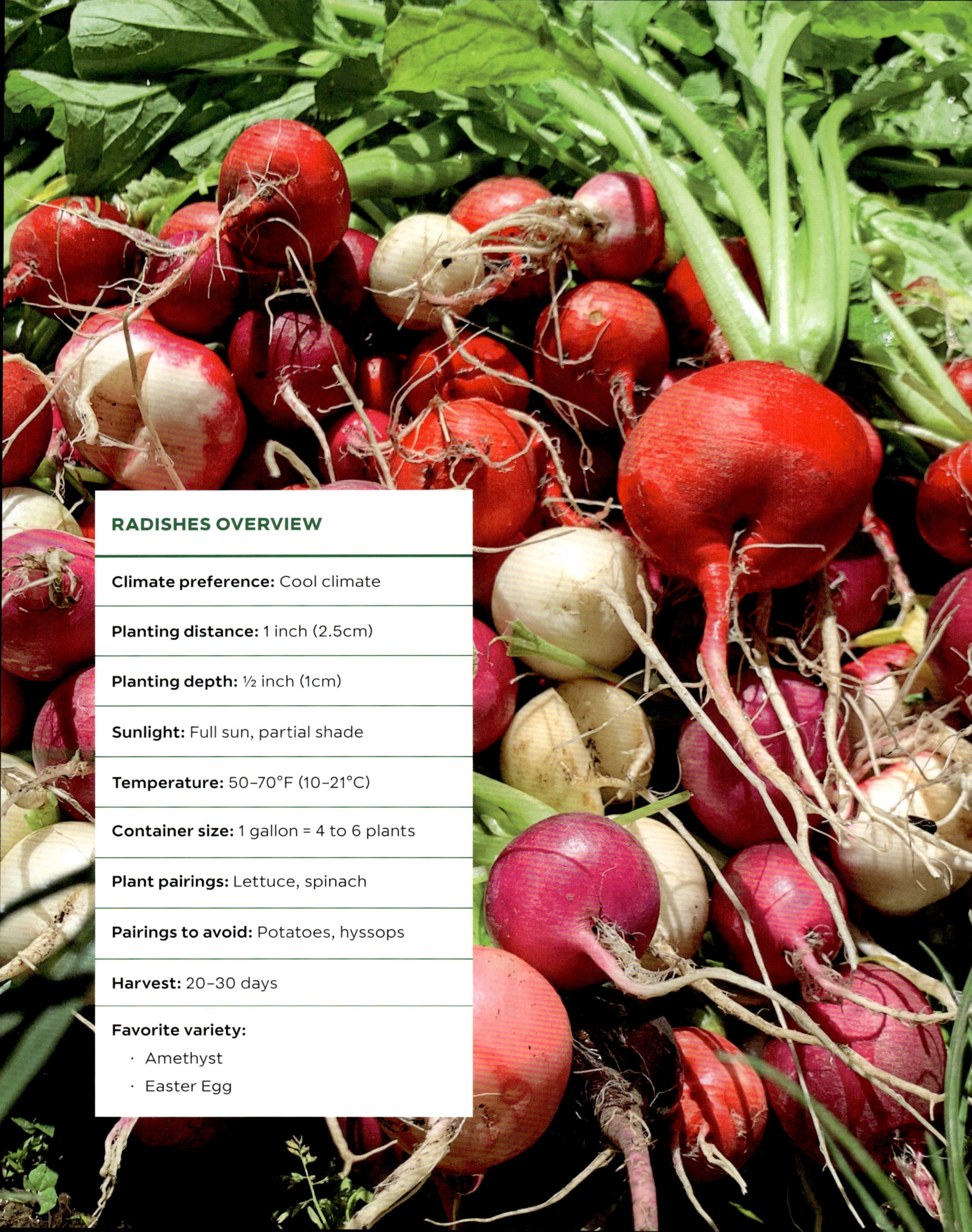

RADISHES OVERVIEW

Climate preference: Cool climate

Planting distance: 1 inch (2.5cm)

Planting depth: ½ inch (1cm)

Sunlight: Full sun, partial shade

Temperature: 50–70°F (10–21°C)

Container size: 1 gallon = 4 to 6 plants

Plant pairings: Lettuce, spinach

Pairings to avoid: Potatoes, hyssops

Harvest: 20–30 days

Favorite variety:
· Amethyst
· Easter Egg

RADISHES

We found that our radishes only produced lush green leaves without forming the roots we wanted. One day, we accidentally dropped a radish seed on gravel, and it ended up growing into a perfect radish! This made us realize that growing radishes didn't have to be complicated. We just needed to improve our soil at the end of the season and plant the seeds in early spring. This simple change led to a great harvest.

Planting Radishes 101

In spring, you can plant seeds when the temperatures are between 50 and 70°F (10 and 21°C). For a fall harvest, plant them about 4 to 6 weeks before the first frost. Radishes grow best when directly sown, as their delicate roots don't do well when moved. Choose a sunny spot with loose, well-draining soil with a layer of compost. To plant, make a shallow line in the soil (we use a wooden stick), and place the seeds about ½ inch (1cm) deep. Plant seeds 1 inch (2.5cm) apart. Radishes grow quickly and usually sprout within 3 to 7 days. Keep the soil moist during this time to help them grow fast.

Growing Radishes 101

Radishes are light feeders and don't need a lot of fertilizer, but adding compost to the soil before planting can give them a healthy start. Avoid using too much nitrogen, as it leads to leafy growth at the expense of the root. Water deeply 2 to 3 times per week.

Growing Radishes in Pots

Use a container that's at least 6 to 8 inches (15 to 20cm) deep to allow room for the roots to develop. A 2- to 3-gallon container is ideal for a small batch of radishes, and you can plant about 4 to 6 radishes per gallon of soil. Fill the container with a well-draining potting mix, add compost, and water deeply.

Optional Amendments

· **Compost:** Mix into the soil before planting.

Challenges

Pests such as flea beetles, slugs, and root maggots are common problems. Flea beetles and slugs chew on the leaves, while root maggots attack the roots. To prevent pests, cover the plants with a floating row cover. You can also plant nasturtiums or chives nearby to keep pests away and attract helpful insects.

SPINACH

Spinach thrives in cool weather and grows quickly. We love planting the Bloomsdale variety in the cool spring months. As the weather warms up, we switch to New Zealand spinach and Malabar spinach. While these are technically not true spinach, they have a similar taste and grow wonderfully in the heat of summer.

Planting Spinach 101

In general, spinach is grown in early spring or fall. If you're in a colder region, plant as soon as the ground is workable in spring, 4 to 6 weeks before the last frost date. In warm climates, fall planting works well since spinach tolerates light frosts and cooler weather. Spinach plants prefer well-drained, nutrient-rich soil, so mix in compost or aged manure before planting. Sow the seeds about ½ inch (1cm) deep. Standard spacing is 3 to 4 inches (7.5 to 10cm) apart. We like to space ours at 2 inches (5cm) apart. Keep in mind that closer spacing may result in slightly smaller leaves but allows you to grow more plants in less space.

Growing Spinach 101

Water regularly, keeping the soil evenly moist. Feed your spinach plants with natural amendments like compost tea or compost every 2 to 3 weeks. Nitrogen is especially important because it promotes lush, leafy growth. Consider using shade cloth during hot afternoons to prevent the plants from bolting.

Growing Spinach in Pots

Choose a container that is at least 6 to 8 inches (15 to 20cm) deep, as spinach has relatively shallow roots. A 3-gallon container is ideal for growing about 5 plants. Make sure your pot has good drainage holes, use potting mix with compost, and place the container in a spot that gets at least 4 to 6 hours of sunlight daily.

Optional Amendments

- **Compost:** Mix into the soil before planting to improve fertility and structure.

Challenges

Aphids and leaf miners are the most common pests for spinach. If you spot aphids, spray the leaves with water. For leaf miners, remove any affected leaves immediately to prevent the larvae from spreading. To prevent pests from the outset, grow spinach under a lightweight row cover. You can plant garlic, onions, and marigolds nearby to keep pests away and attract beneficial bugs.

SPINACH OVERVIEW

Climate preference: Cool climate

Planting distance:
- Standard: 3–4 inches (7.5–10cm)
- Compact: 2 inches (5cm)

Planting depth: ½ inch (1cm)

Sunlight: Full sun, partial shade

Temperature: 50–70°F (10–21°C)

Container size: 3 gallons = 5 plants

Plant pairings: Radishes, carrots

Pairings to avoid: Potatoes

Harvest: 30–55 days

Favorite variety:
- Bloomsdale
- Tyee

SQUASH OVERVIEW

Climate preference: Warm climate

Planting distance:
- **Bush squash**
  Standard: 18–24 inches (45–60cm)
  Compact: 12 inches (30cm)
- **Vine squash**
  Standard: 24–36 inches (60–90cm)
  Compact: 12 inches (30cm)

Planting depth: 1 inch (2.5cm)

Sunlight: Full sun

Temperature: 70–85°F (21–29°C)

Container size: 10 gallons = 1 plant

Plant pairings: Corn, beans, catnip

Pairings to avoid: Potatoes

Harvest:
- Summer: 50–70 days
- Winter: 80–120 days

Favorite variety:
- Red Kuri
- Delicata
- Cue Ball

SQUASH

There are two types of squash to enjoy: summer squash and winter squash. Summer squash, like zucchini and yellow squash, is picked when still young and tender. Winter squash, such as red kuri and acorn squash, is harvested later when the skin is hard, which allows us to store it for months and savor its sweet, hearty flavors in the winter.

Planting Squash 101

Squash loves warm weather and is best planted when the soil is at least 60°F (15°C). Choose a sunny spot that gets 6 to 8 hours of sunlight, and add a layer of compost. Plant the seeds 1 inch (2.5cm) deep, spacing them 24 to 36 inches (60 to 90cm) apart for vining varieties or 18 to 24 inches (45 to 60cm) apart for bush varieties. In a compact garden, you can space them 12 inches (30cm) apart, but be ready to manage the vines to prevent overcrowding. We like to start seeds indoors 3 to 4 weeks before our last frost date. Plant the seeds 1 inch (2.5cm) deep, water lightly, and place under grow lights. Once outdoor soil is warm enough, transplant them into the garden. Be gentle with the seedlings, as squash plants don't like their roots disturbed. Dig a hole big enough for the root ball, and plant them at the same depth they were growing indoors.

Growing Squash 101

To grow healthy squash, consistently water them deeply 2 to 3 times per week, especially during dry spells, and always water at the base to keep the leaves dry and prevent diseases. Squash plants thrive on nutrients, so feed them with compost every 3 to 4 weeks. When the first flowers bloom, start feeding with a high-phosphorus amendment like bone meal. You can help pollinate by gently transferring pollen from male to female flowers. As the vines grow, use trellises to support them vertically, which saves space and improves airflow.

Growing Squash in Pots

Choose a container that's at least 10 gallons; a 15-gallon container is even better for vining varieties. Make sure the container has good drainage holes. Fill the container with a potting mix and compost. Plant 1 to 2 seeds or 1 seedling per container and provide a trellis or stake for vining types to climb. Water deeply.

Optional Amendments

- **Compost:** Mix into the soil at planting and add more every 3 to 4 weeks.
- **Bone meal:** Apply when planting and again when the plant starts to flower.
- **Fish emulsion:** Use every 2 weeks during the first month of growth to encourage strong, leafy vines.

Challenges

Pests like squash bugs or vine borers can damage your crops. Inspect your plants regularly, handpick pests, and use row covers to protect young plants. Powdery mildew, a common fungal disease, can be prevented by improving air circulation around the plants and watering at the base. If overcrowding is an issue, prune excess leaves.

TOMATOES

With over ten thousand types of tomatoes, the first step is choosing which one to grow. They come in different sizes: micro dwarf, dwarf, determinate, and indeterminate. The key difference is that indeterminate tomatoes keep growing and producing fruit all season, while determinate tomatoes grow to a set height and produce all their fruit at once.

Planting Tomatoes 101

If planting seeds directly, wait until the soil is at least 60°F (15°C), which is usually a few weeks after your last frost date in the spring. Choose a sunny spot with good, well-draining soil. Sow seeds ¼ inch (0.5cm) deep, with standard spacing at 24 to 36 inches (60 to 90cm) apart for full-size plants. For small spaces, you can plant them 18 inches (45cm) apart, but be ready to support and prune them to avoid overcrowding. Start seeds indoors 6 to 8 weeks before the last frost date. Plant 2 seeds per hole about ¼ inch (0.5cm) deep. When the seedlings are big enough, move them to 5-inch (12.5cm) containers, and water from the bottom. Once they're 6 to 8 inches (15 to 20cm) tall, they're ready to transplant. Harden off the seedlings by gradually exposing them to outdoor conditions over a week, then transplant them when the soil is warm and nighttime temperatures are consistently above 50°F (10°C).

Growing Tomatoes 101

Choose a spot where they'll get at least 6 to 8 hours of sunlight daily. Water them deeply 2 to 3 times per week. Before planting, amend the soil with compost. During the growing season, feed them every 3 to 4 weeks with chicken-manure granules or fish emulsion. As your tomato plants grow, they'll need support to keep the fruits off the ground.

Growing Tomatoes in Pots

Choose a container that's at least 10 gallons, with a minimum depth of 12 inches (30cm) for each plant. For determinate tomatoes, you can get away with a 5-gallon pot. Fill the container with potting mix and make sure it has drainage holes to prevent water from pooling. Water deeply and fertilize every 2 to 3 weeks with chicken-manure granules or fish emulsion. Chicken-manure granules contain calcium and can prevent blossom-end rot.

Optional Amendments

- **Chicken-manure granules:** Apply when first planting and then again every 3 to 4 weeks.
- **Fish emulsion:** Best applied every 3 to 4 weeks throughout the growing season.
- **Compost:** Mix in before planting and then side dress with more every 4 to 6 weeks.

Challenges

Pests like aphids, tomato hornworms, and whiteflies are common. To control them, use insecticidal soap and handpick larger pests, or introduce beneficial insects like ladybugs. Diseases like blight, fusarium wilt, and powdery mildew can affect tomatoes. To prevent these, space the plants properly for good air circulation, avoid overhead watering, and rotate crops each year to prevent soil-borne diseases. Companion-plant with basil, marigolds, or garlic to help repel pests and improve growth.

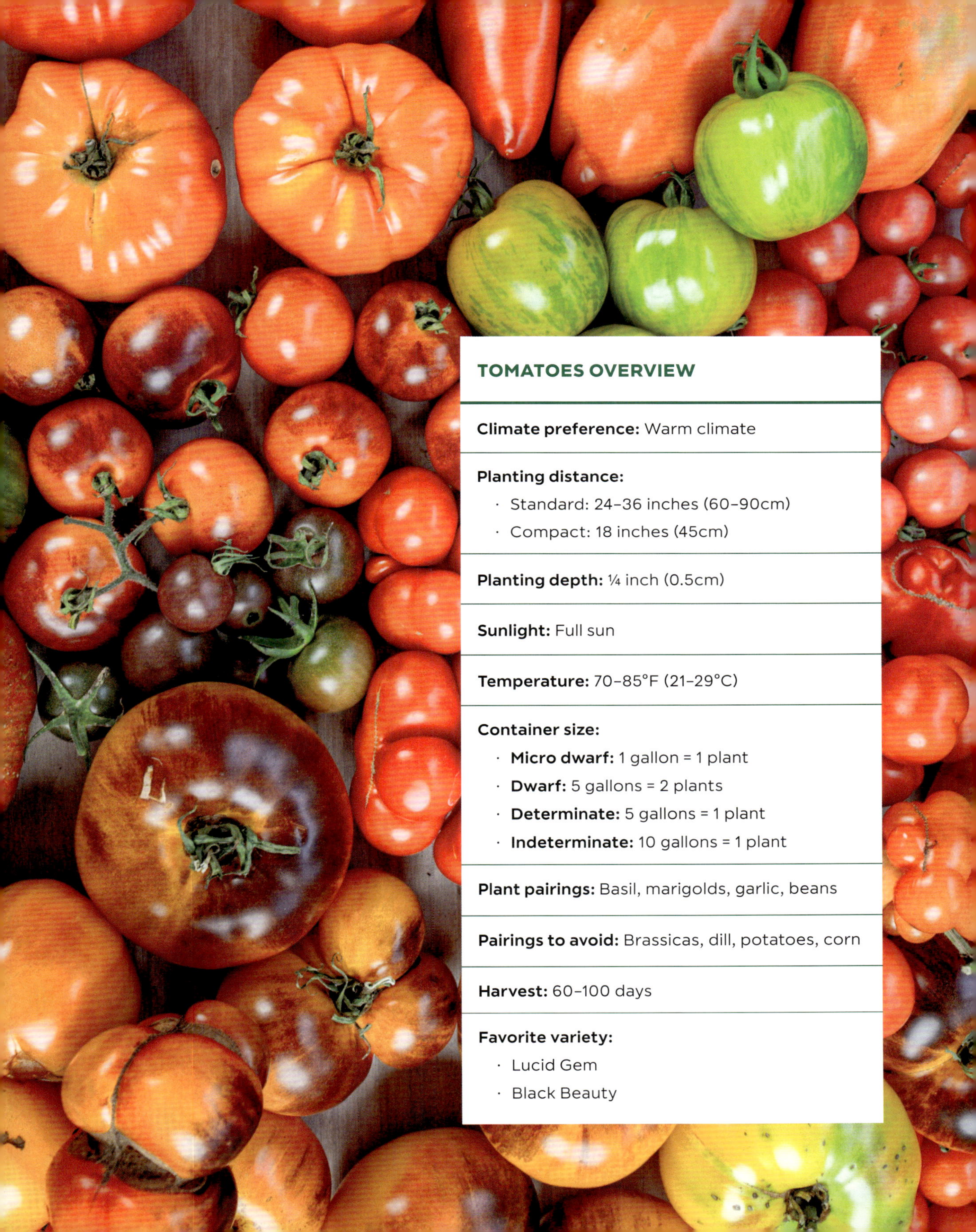

TOMATOES OVERVIEW

Climate preference: Warm climate

Planting distance:
· Standard: 24–36 inches (60–90cm)
· Compact: 18 inches (45cm)

Planting depth: ¼ inch (0.5cm)

Sunlight: Full sun

Temperature: 70–85°F (21–29°C)

Container size:
· Micro dwarf: 1 gallon = 1 plant
· Dwarf: 5 gallons = 2 plants
· Determinate: 5 gallons = 1 plant
· Indeterminate: 10 gallons = 1 plant

Plant pairings: Basil, marigolds, garlic, beans

Pairings to avoid: Brassicas, dill, potatoes, corn

Harvest: 60–100 days

Favorite variety:
· Lucid Gem
· Black Beauty

FLOWER PROFILES

BEE BALM

Bee balm is a colorful flower that not only beautifies your garden but also has medicinal properties. It has been traditionally used to make teas and is believed to aid in digestion and to relieve cold symptoms.

Climate preference: Temperate climate

Planting distance:

- Standard: 18–24 inches (45–60cm)
- Compact: 10–12 inches (25–30cm)

Planting depth: ¼ inch (0.5cm)

Sunlight: Full sun, partial shade

Temperature: 70–85°F (21–29°C)

Container size: 5 gallons = 1 plant

Plant pairings: Squash, zucchini

Pairings to avoid: Corn, tomatoes

Harvest: 60–90 days

Benefits: Bee balm smells sweet and attracts bees, butterflies, and hummingbirds. It is easy to grow; has edible leaves and flowers; and is often used in teas and salads. Remove old blooms to encourage new ones and be aware that it spreads quickly.

CALENDULA

Calendula is one of the easiest flowers to grow in the garden, and it blooms all summer long, growing quickly from seeds.

Climate preference: Cool climate

Planting distance:

- Standard: 8–12 inches (20–30cm)
- Compact: 4–6 inches (10–15cm)

Planting depth: ¼ inch (0.5cm)

Sunlight: Full sun, partial shade

Temperature: 60–70°F (15–21°C)

Container size: 5 gallons = 2 to 3 plants

Plant pairings: Tomatoes, beans, cucumbers

Harvest: 45–60 days

Benefits: Calendula flowers help keep pests like aphids and whiteflies away and attract helpful bugs like ladybugs and hoverflies, making them great for your garden. Remember not to overwater them and to trim off spent flowers to encourage more blooms.

DAHLIA

Dahlias are breathtaking flowers that come in many colors and shapes, our favorite variety being Ferncliff Dolly. In cool climates, you need to carefully remove the tubers in the fall and store them in a cool, dry place to protect them from freezing. We replant them in the spring to enjoy their beauty all over again.

Climate preference: Warm climate
Planting distance:
  · Standard: 18–24 inches (45–60cm)
  · Compact: 10–12 inches (25–30cm)
Planting depth: 4–6 inches (10–15cm)
Sunlight: Full sun
Temperature: 60–70°F (15–21°C)
Container size: 5 gallons = 1 plant
Plant pairings: Tomatoes, eggplants, squash
Pairings to avoid: Potatoes
Harvest: 60–90 days
Benefits: Dahlias attract helpful insects like bees and butterflies and add bright colors to your garden, but be careful not to overwater them and watch out for slugs and snails that might eat the young plants.

ECHINACEA

Echinacea is a beautiful plant that adds color to your garden while attracting bees, ladybugs, and butterflies. Growing echinacea is a great choice because it's easy to care for and brings both beauty and beneficial pollinators to your outdoor space.

Climate preference: Temperate climate
Planting distance:
  · Standard: 18–24 inches (45–60cm)
  · Compact: 10–12 inches (25–30cm)
Planting depth: ¼ inch (0.5cm)
Sunlight: Full sun, partial shade
Temperature: 55–75°F (13–24°C)
Container size: 5 gallons = 1 to 2 plants
Plant pairings: Tomatoes, peppers
Harvest: 90–120 days
Benefits: Echinacea attracts helpful insects like bees and butterflies that keep pests away. Plant it in well-draining soil with plenty of sunlight, and avoid overwatering.

LAVENDER

Lavender brings beautiful color and a wonderful scent while attracting helpful bugs like bees, butterflies, ladybugs, and lacewings and keeping away pesky pests like mosquitoes, flies, aphids, and spider mites.

Climate preference: Temperate climate
Planting distance:
- Standard: 18–24 inches (45–60cm)
- Compact: 10–12 inches (25–30cm)

Planting depth: ½ inch (1cm)
Sunlight: Full sun
Temperature: 60–80°F (15–26°C)
Container size: 5 gallons = 1 plant
Plant pairings: Rosemary, sage, thyme, tomatoes
Pairings to avoid: Lettuce
Harvest: 90–120 days
Benefits: Lavender helps keep away pests like mosquitoes and flies while attracting helpful pollinators like bees and butterflies.

MARIGOLD

When we started growing French marigolds in our garden, we saw a big difference because they attracted friendly bugs and kept harmful pests away.

Climate preference: Warm climate
Planting distance:
- Standard: 10–12 inches (25–30cm)
- Compact: 6–8 inches (15–20cm)

Planting depth: ¼ inch (0.5cm)
Sunlight: Full sun
Temperature: 70–75°F (21–24°C)
Container size: 2 gallons = 1 plant
Plant pairings: Tomatoes, peppers, cucumbers
Pairings to avoid: Beans, cabbage
Harvest: 60 days
Benefits: Marigolds keep away pests like aphids, whiteflies, and mosquitoes while attracting helpful bugs like bees and butterflies.

NASTURTIUMS

Nasturtiums are the perfect trap crop for any garden because they attract pests away from your other plants, helping to keep them safe. Plus, you can enjoy their beautiful flowers, leaves, and green seed pods, all of which have a tasty peppery flavor.

Climate preference: Cool climate
Planting distance:

- Standard: 10–12 inches (25–30cm)
- Compact: 6–8 inches (15–20cm)

Planting depth: ½ inch (1cm)
Sunlight: Full sun, partial shade
Temperature: 55–70°F (13–21°C)
Container size: 5 gallons = 3 to 4 plants
Plant pairings: Tomatoes, cucumbers, kale
Pairings to avoid: Potatoes
Harvest: 60–70 days
Benefits: Nasturtiums keep away pests like aphids, squash bugs, cucumber beetles, and whiteflies while attracting helpful bugs like bees and ladybugs. Plant them in poor soil; they thrive in less fertile conditions, which encourages more vibrant blooms and helps keep them healthy!

SUNFLOWERS

Sunflowers invite beneficial bugs and predatory insects into your balanced ecosystem, making your garden healthier. The only challenge is trying to get those sunflowers fully grown before the squirrels and birds get to them!

Climate preference: Warm climate
Planting distance:

- Standard: 18–24 inches (45–60cm)
- Compact: 10–12 inches (25–30cm)

Planting depth: 1–2 inches (2.5–5cm)
Sunlight: Full sun
Temperature: 70–78°F (21–25°C)
Container size: 5 gallons = 2 to 3 plants (smaller varieties)
Plant pairings: Corn, squash, beans
Pairings to avoid: Potatoes, pole beans
Harvest: 80–120 days
Benefits: Sunflowers are not only beautiful, but they also keep pests like aphids away and attract helpful birds that eat those pests, as well as pollinators like bees and butterflies. We like to use the dried stalks the next growing season as stakes for vining plants.

ZINNIA

Zinnias are beautiful, reliable bushy flowers that look like little pom-poms and come in a rainbow of colors, including red, pink, orange, yellow, and white. They're easy to grow and make great cut flowers that last a long time, so we plant them every year without fail.

Climate preference: Warm climate
Planting distance:
- Standard: 10–12 inches (25–30cm)
- Compact: 6–8 inches (15–20cm)

Planting depth: ¼ inch (0.5cm)
Sunlight: Full sun
Temperature: 70–85°F (21–29°C)
Container size: 5 gallons = 6 to 8 plants
Plant pairings: Tomatoes, cucumbers, basil
Pairings to avoid: Squash, pumpkins
Harvest: 60–70 days
Benefits: Zinnias attract helpful insects like ladybugs and bees and naturally draw predatory insects like lacewings and parasitic wasps. They're easy to care for but just remember to remove spent blooms to keep them blooming all season long.

HERB PROFILES

BASIL

It's a must-have herb for any garden! We grow it year-round in Canada, even in the winter, using hydroponics. We grow different types, such as Genovese for pesto and Thai basil for soup.

Climate preference: Warm climate
Planting distance:
- Standard: 12 inches (30cm)
- Compact: 6 inches (15cm)

Planting depth: ¼–½ inch (0.5–1cm)
Sunlight: Full sun
Temperature: 70–90°F (21–32°C)
Container size:
- 5 gallons = 2 to 3 plants
- 10 gallons = 3 to 4 plants

Plant pairings: Tomatoes, peppers, oregano
Pairings to avoid: Cucumbers, sage, fennel
Harvest: 50–90 days
Benefits: The combo of basil, tomatoes, and marigolds is the dream team: Marigolds keep unwanted pests away and basil boosts tomato growth.

CILANTRO

Cilantro usually bolts in the summer, leaving us without it during the best salsa-making time. Luckily, we found a slow-bolting type called Calypso and learned about succession planting; so with a little planning, we can have fresh cilantro whenever we need it.

Climate preference: Cool climate
Planting distance:
- Standard: 6–8 inches (15–20cm)
- Compact: 4 inches (10cm)

Planting depth: ¼ inch (0.5cm)
Sunlight: Full sun, partial shade
Temperature: 50–85°F (10–29°C)
Container size: 2–3 gallons = 8 to 10 plants
Plant pairings: Tomatoes, carrots, spinach, basil
Pairings to avoid: Fennel
Harvest: 50–55 days
Benefits: Cilantro attracts helpful pest-eating insects like parasitic wasps, ladybugs, and lacewings. Plus, it keeps away harmful bugs like aphids, making your garden healthier.

DILL

Dill grows really well alongside plants like cucumbers and cabbage because it helps keep pests away while they grow. Plus, it's easy to care for, so you can enjoy its delicious taste right from your garden.

Climate preference: Cool climate
Planting distance:
- Standard: 8–12 inches (20–30cm)
- Compact: 6 inches (15cm)

Planting depth: ¼–½ inch (0.5–1cm)
Sunlight: Full sun
Temperature: 60–70°F (15–21°C)
Container size: 5 gallons = 8 to 10 plants
Plant pairings: Cabbage, corn, cucumbers
Pairings to avoid: Carrots, tomatoes
Harvest: 40–60 days
Benefits: Dill repels pests like aphids, spider mites, and cabbage worms while attracting beneficial insects like ladybugs and lacewings, which prey on these pests, helping to keep your garden healthy and balanced.

LEMONGRASS

Lemongrass is a fragrant plant that's easy to grow; instead of starting from seed, we use root stalks: Soak them in water to help them sprout, then transplant them into the soil after the last frost date.

Climate preference: Warm climate
Planting distance:
- Standard: 10–12 inches (25–30cm)
- Compact: 6–8 inches (15–20cm)

Planting depth: 1–2 inches (2.5–5cm)
Sunlight: Full sun
Temperature: 70–85°F (21–29°C)
Container size: 5 gallons = 2 to 3 plants
Plant pairings: Basil, cilantro, mint
Pairings to avoid: Brassicas
Harvest: 90–120 days
Benefits: Lemongrass deters pests like mosquitoes. In the kitchen, it's used in teas, soups, curries, and marinades.

OREGANO

Oregano is low maintenance, loves sunny places with good soil, and is easy to grow.

Climate preference: Warm climate
Planting distance:
- Standard: 10–12 inches (25–30cm)
- Compact: 6–8 inches (15–20cm)

Planting depth: ¼ inch (0.5cm)
Sunlight: Full sun, partial shade
Temperature: 70°F (21°C)
Container size: 1 gallon = 1 plant
Plant pairings: Tomatoes, peppers
Pairings to avoid: Fennel
Harvest: 60–90 days
Benefits: Oregano attracts beneficial insects like bees and butterflies, which help pollinate other plants. It also keeps away pests like aphids and cabbage moths, making your garden healthier and more productive.

PARSLEY

Parsley is a delicious green herb packed with iron and is very easy to grow.

Climate preference: Cool climate
Planting distance:
- Standard: 8–12 inches (20–30cm)
- Compact: 6–8 inches (15–20cm)

Planting depth: ¼–½ inch (0.5–1cm)
Sunlight: Full sun, partial shade
Temperature: 70°F (21°C)
Container size: 1 gallon = 1 plant
Plant pairings: Tomatoes, peppers, carrots
Pairings to avoid: Sage
Harvest: 70–90 days
Benefits: Parsley attracts helpful bugs like bees and butterflies and helps keep away pests like aphids and cabbage moths, making your garden healthier and more productive. Be careful not to overwater, as parsley prefers slightly moist soil.

ROSEMARY

Rosemary is a tough plant that can grow in many types of climates.

Climate preference: Temperate climate
Planting distance:
  · Standard: 18–24 inches (45–60cm)
  · Compact: 12–15 inches (30–38cm)
Planting depth: ¼ inch (0.5cm)
Sunlight: Full sun, partial shade
Temperature: 50–85°F (10–29°C)
Container size: 3 gallons = 1 plant
Plant pairings: Tomatoes, carrots, cabbages
Pairings to avoid: Lettuce
Harvest: 70–90 days
Benefits: Rosemary attracts helpful bugs like bees and butterflies, while also keeping away unwanted pests like mosquitoes and cabbage moths. Rosemary grows best with vegetables like carrots and cabbage because it improves their flavor and keeps them healthy.

SAGE

Sage is one of the best herbs for drying, as it retains its delicious flavor. To keep your sage plant looking bushy and healthy, pinch off new shoots regularly.

Climate preference: Warm climate
Planting distance:
  · Standard: 18–24 inches (45–60cm)
  · Compact: 12–15 inches (30–38cm)
Planting depth: ¼ inch (0.5cm)
Sunlight: Full sun, partial shade
Temperature: 60–70°F (15–21°C)
Container size: 3 gallons = 1 plant
Plant pairings: Rosemary, carrots, cabbages
Pairings to avoid: Cucumbers
Harvest: 70–90 days
Benefits: Sage deters pests like cabbage moths and attracts beneficial bugs like bees.

THYME

Growing thyme is easy because it requires very little moisture and dislikes being overwatered. This hardy herb loves full sun, so make sure to plant it in a bright spot in your garden to enjoy its many benefits!

Climate preference: Warm climate
Planting distance:
  · Standard: 10–12 inches (25–30cm)
  · Compact: 6–8 inches (15–20cm)
Planting depth: ¼ inch (0.5cm)
Sunlight: Full sun
Temperature: 60–70°F (15–21°C)
Container size: 1 gallon = 1 plant
Plant pairings: Rosemary, cabbage, tomatoes
Pairings to avoid: Basil
Harvest: 70–90 days
Benefits: Thyme deters pests like cabbage worms and attracts beneficial insects like bees and ladybugs that help control aphid populations.

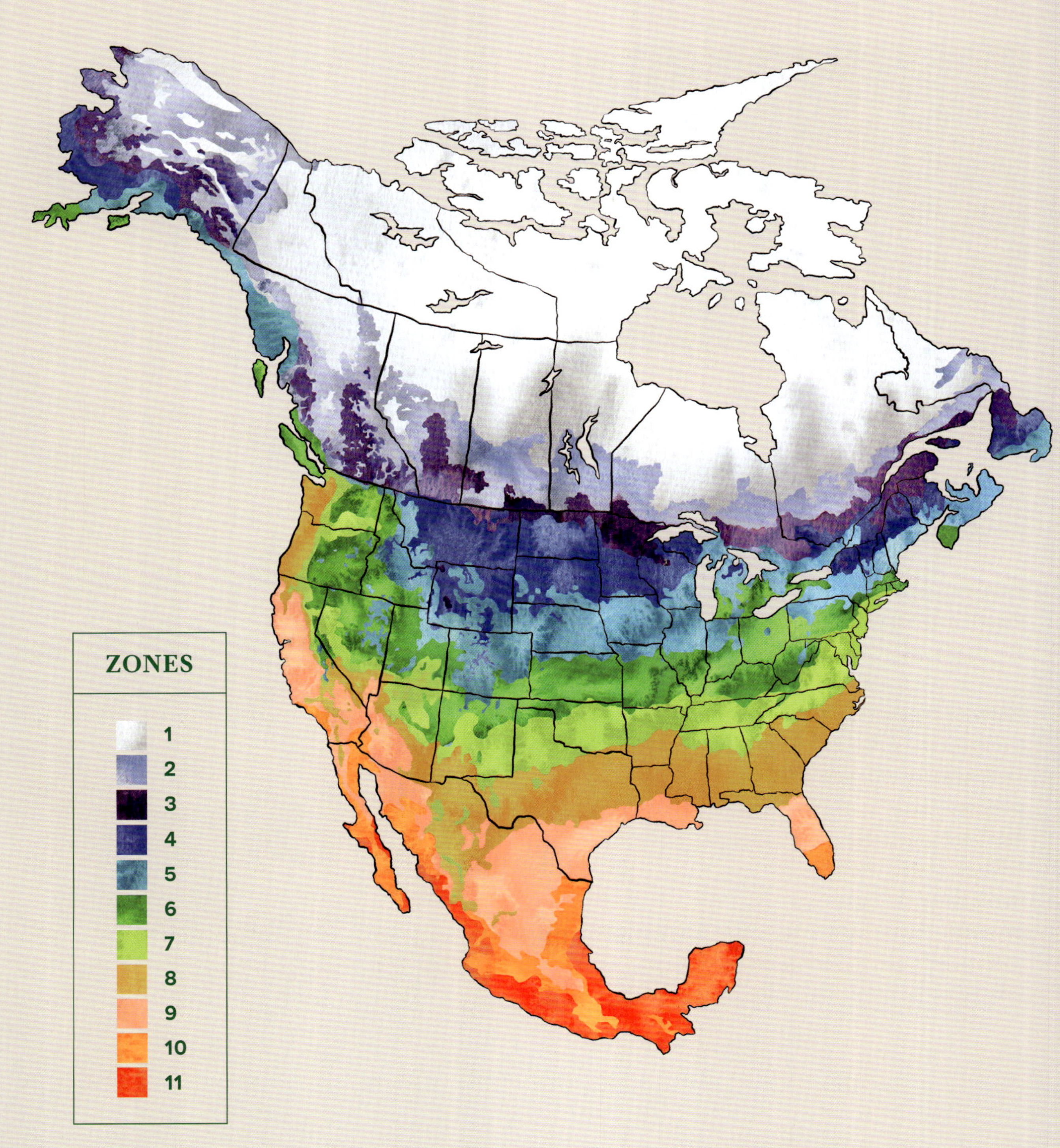

ZONES
1
2
3
4
5
6
7
8
9
10
11

PLANTING CALENDARS & SCHEDULES

This section will help you understand when best to begin planting your many treasures. The term "direct sowing" means planting seeds directly into your garden soil where they'll grow to maturity—think of scattering bean seeds in a row or poking sunflower seeds into the ground. Transplanting involves starting seeds indoors first, nurturing them into small plants, then moving these seedlings outside once conditions are right. Transplanting gives temperature-sensitive crops such as tomatoes and peppers a head start on the growing season. Finally, "hardiness zones" are your secret weapon for selecting plants that will survive your local winters. These zones, numbered 1 through 11, correspond with the temperature of your area, with lower zone numbers indicating colder regions. When you see "zones 5–9" on a plant tag, it means the plant can tolerate winter temperatures down to zone 5's bitter cold but will not survive anything colder. Understanding your zone helps you make smart choices about what to grow and when to plant. For this planting calendar, we've focused on zones 3 through 10, which represent the most common gardening regions around the world.

ZONE 3
(−40°F TO −30°F)
(−40°C TO −34°C)

Growing season:

90–120 days

Last spring frost:

May 15–June 1

First fall frost:

September 15–
October 1

— Direct Sow

— Indoor Seed Starting

— Transplant

Special Considerations

• Extremely short seasons require quick-maturing varieties

• Use season extension (row covers, cold frames) extensively

• Focus on cold-hardy varieties

PLANTING CALENDAR

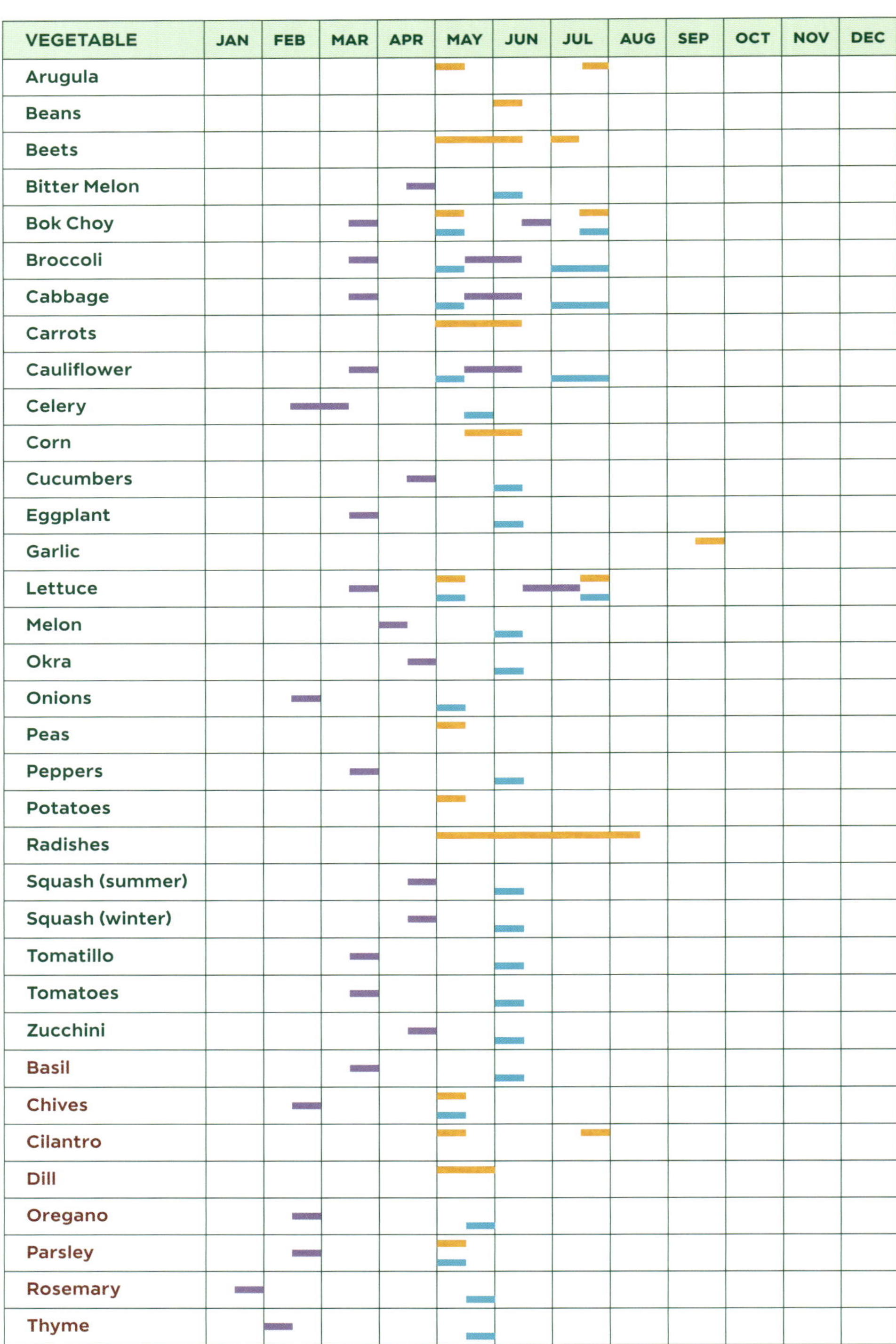

Legend: **DS** = Direct Sow (orange), **ISS** = Indoor Seed Starting (purple), **TP** = Transplant (blue)

VEGETABLE	JAN	FEB	MAR	APR	MAY	JUN	JUL	AUG	SEP	OCT	NOV	DEC
Arugula					DS		DS					
Beans						DS						
Beets					DS	DS	DS					
Bitter Melon				ISS		TP						
Bok Choy			ISS		DS	ISS	DS					
			TP				TP					
Broccoli			ISS		TP	ISS	TP					
Cabbage			ISS		TP	ISS	TP					
Carrots					DS	DS						
Cauliflower			ISS		TP	ISS	TP					
Celery		ISS	ISS		TP							
Corn					DS							
Cucumbers				ISS		TP						
Eggplant			ISS			TP						
Garlic									DS			
Lettuce			ISS		DS/TP	ISS	DS/TP					
Melon				ISS		TP						
Okra				ISS		TP						
Onions		ISS			TP							
Peas					DS							
Peppers			ISS			TP						
Potatoes					DS							
Radishes					DS	DS	DS	DS				
Squash (summer)				ISS		TP						
Squash (winter)				ISS		TP						
Tomatillo			ISS			TP						
Tomatoes			ISS			TP						
Zucchini				ISS		TP						
Basil			ISS			TP						
Chives		ISS			DS/TP							
Cilantro					DS		DS					
Dill					DS							
Oregano			ISS		TP							
Parsley			ISS		DS/TP							
Rosemary		ISS				TP						
Thyme		ISS	ISS			TP						

MONTHLY PLANTING SCHEDULE

January
- Planning and seed ordering
- Prepare seed-starting equipment
- **Indoor seed starting (mid-January):** long-season herbs like rosemary and thyme

February
- **Indoor seed starting (mid-February):** celery, onions, chives, oregano, parsley

March
- **Indoor seed starting (mid-March):** bok choy, broccoli, cabbage, cauliflower, lettuce for spring transplants
- **Indoor seed starting (mid-March):** eggplant, peppers, tomatillo, tomatoes, basil for summer transplants

April
- **Indoor seed starting (early-April):** melon
- **Indoor seed starting (mid-April):** bitter melon, cucumber, okra, squash, zucchini

May
- Wait for soil to warm and plant only if soil is workable
- **Direct sow (early-May):** arugula, beets, bok choy, carrots, lettuce, peas, potatoes, radishes, chives, cilantro, dill, parsley
- **Transplant (early-May):** bok choy, broccoli, cabbage, cauliflower, lettuce, chives, parsley if started indoors
- **Transplant (mid-May):** celery, oregano, rosemary, thyme

June
- **Direct sow (early-June):** beans, corn
- **Transplant:** all warm-season crops after June 1
- **Indoor seed starting (early-June):** broccoli, cabbage, cauliflower
- **Indoor seed starting (mid-June):** bok choy, lettuce for succession planting

July
- Final plantings of quick crops
- Begin succession planting for continuous harvest
- **Direct sow (mid-July):** arugula, bok choy, lettuce, radishes, cilantro
- **Transplant (early to mid-July):** bok choy, broccoli, cabbage, cauliflower, lettuce if started indoors

August
- **Direct sow (early-August only):** final radishes
- Harvest begins for early crops

September–December
- **Direct sow (mid-September):** garlic cloves
- Focus: harvesting, preserving, remove spent plants, add 2-4 inches compost, plant cover crops, mulch
- Start microgreens and indoor garden
- Plan next year's garden

HIGH DENSITY 4X8 FT GARDEN BED PLAN

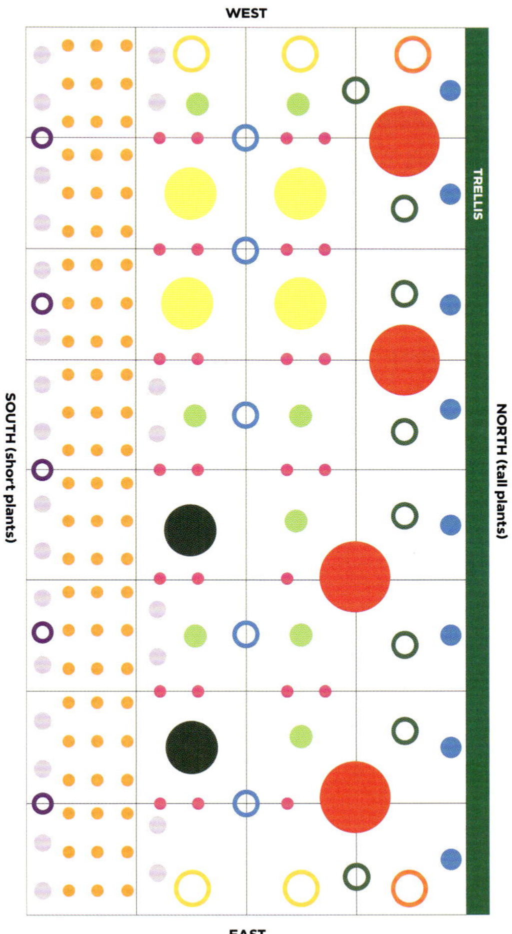

PLANTING SCHEDULE

COOL SEASON	WARM SEASON
Carrots (72)	Basil (8)
Lettuce (8)	Cucumbers (2)
Onions (24)	French Marigold (2)
Radishes (26)	Nasturtiums (4)
Chives (5)	Peppers (4)
Parsley (5)	Pole Beans (8)
	Tomatoes (4)

ZONE 4
(–30°F TO –20°F)
(–34°C TO –29°C)

Growing season:

120–150 days

Last spring frost:

May 1–May 15

First fall frost:

October 1–
October 15

— Direct Sow

— Indoor Seed Starting

— Transplant

Special Considerations

- Still requires quick-maturing varieties

- Season extension beneficial

- Focus on frost-tolerant varieties for fall

PLANTING CALENDAR

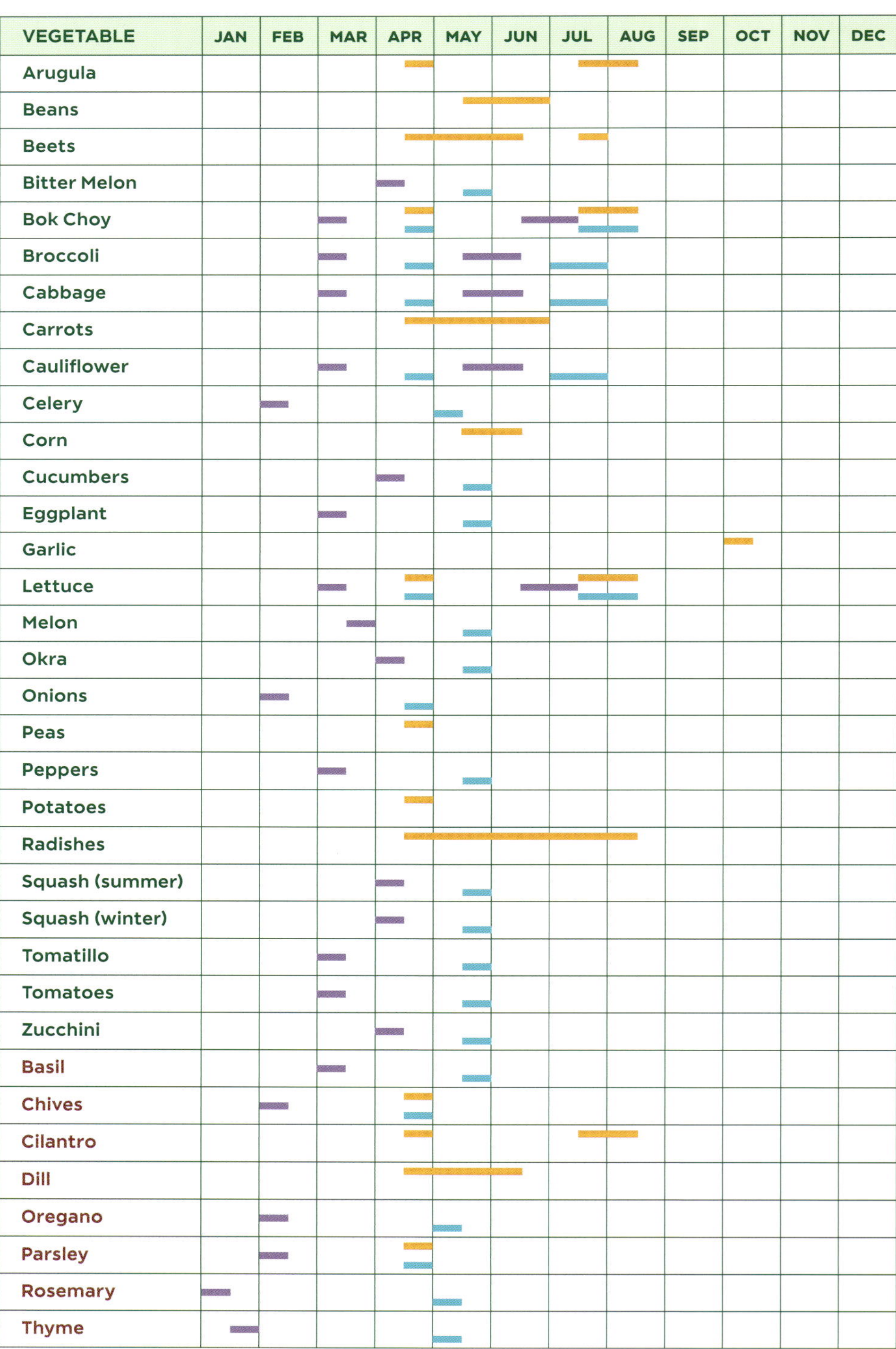

Legend: DS = Direct Sow · IS = Indoor Seed Starting · T = Transplant

VEGETABLE	JAN	FEB	MAR	APR	MAY	JUN	JUL	AUG	SEP	OCT	NOV	DEC
Arugula				DS			DS	DS				
Beans					DS	DS						
Beets				DS	DS	DS	DS					
Bitter Melon				IS	T							
Bok Choy			IS	DS, T		IS	DS, T	DS, T				
Broccoli			IS		T	IS						
Cabbage			IS		T	IS						
Carrots				DS	DS	DS						
Cauliflower			IS		T	IS						
Celery		IS			T							
Corn					DS	DS						
Cucumbers				IS	T							
Eggplant			IS		T							
Garlic										DS		
Lettuce			IS	DS	T	IS	DS, T	DS, T				
Melon			IS		T							
Okra				IS	T							
Onions		IS			T							
Peas				DS								
Peppers			IS		T							
Potatoes				DS								
Radishes				DS	DS	DS	DS	DS				
Squash (summer)				IS	T							
Squash (winter)				IS	T							
Tomatillo			IS		T							
Tomatoes			IS		T							
Zucchini				IS	T							
Basil			IS		T							
Chives		IS		DS	T							
Cilantro				DS			DS					
Dill				DS	DS	DS						
Oregano			IS		T							
Parsley			IS	DS	T							
Rosemary	IS				T							
Thyme		IS			T							

MONTHLY PLANTING SCHEDULE

January
- Planning and seed ordering
- Prepare seed-starting equipment
- **Indoor seed starting (mid-January):** long-season herbs like rosemary and thyme

February
- **Indoor seed starting (early-February):** celery, onions, chives, oregano, parsley

March
- **Indoor seed starting (early-March):** bok choy, broccoli, cabbage, cauliflower, lettuce for spring transplants
- **Indoor seed starting (early-March):** eggplant, peppers, tomatillo, tomatoes, basil for summer transplants
- **Indoor seed starting (mid-March):** melon

April
- **Indoor seed starting (early-April):** bitter melon, cucumber, okra, squash, zucchini
- Wait for soil to warm and plant only if soil is workable
- **Direct sow (mid-April):** arugula, beets, bok choy, carrots, lettuce, peas, potato, radishes, chives, cilantro, dill, parsley
- **Transplant (mid-April):** bok choy, broccoli, cabbage, cauliflower, lettuce, chives, parsley if started indoors

May
- **Transplant (early-May):** celery, oregano, rosemary, thyme
- **Direct sow (mid-May):** beans, corn
- **Transplant (mid-May):** all warm-season crops after soil warms
- **Indoor seed starting (mid-May):** broccoli, cabbage, cauliflower

June
- **Indoor seed starting (mid-June):** bok choy, lettuce for succession planting

July
- Begin succession planting for continuous harvest
- **Direct sow (mid-July):** arugula, beets, bok choy, lettuce, radishes, cilantro
- **Transplant (early- to mid-July):** bok choy, broccoli, cabbage, cauliflower, lettuce if started indoors

August
- **Final plantings of quick crops (early-August):** arugula, bok choy, lettuce, radishes, cilantro
- Begin major harvest period

September–December
- Focus: harvesting, preservation, garden cleanup
- **Direct sow (early-October):** garlic cloves
- Start microgreens and indoor garden
- Plan next year's garden

HIGH DENSITY 4X8 FT GARDEN BED PLAN

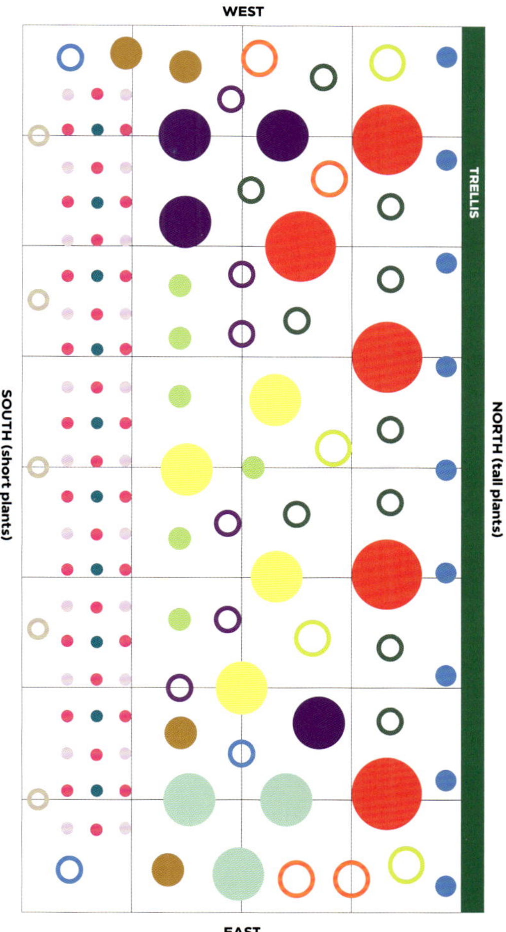

PLANTING SCHEDULE

COOL SEASON
- Beets (22)
- Cilantro (6)
- Lettuce (6)
- Radishes (31)
- Spinach (10)
- Swiss Chard (4)
- Thyme (5)

WARM SEASON
- Basil (10)
- Borage (3)
- Bush Beans (3)
- Calendula (4)
- Eggplants (4)
- Peppers (4)
- Pole Beans (9)
- Tomatoes (5)
- Zinnias (4)

ZONE 5
(–20°F TO –10°F)
(–29°C TO –23°C)

Growing season:

150–180 days

Last spring frost:

April 15–May 1

First fall frost:

October 15–
November 1

─── Direct Sow

─── Indoor Seed Starting

─── Transplant

Special Considerations

• Good balance of cool- and warm-season crops is possible

• Season extension extends harvest significantly

PLANTING CALENDAR

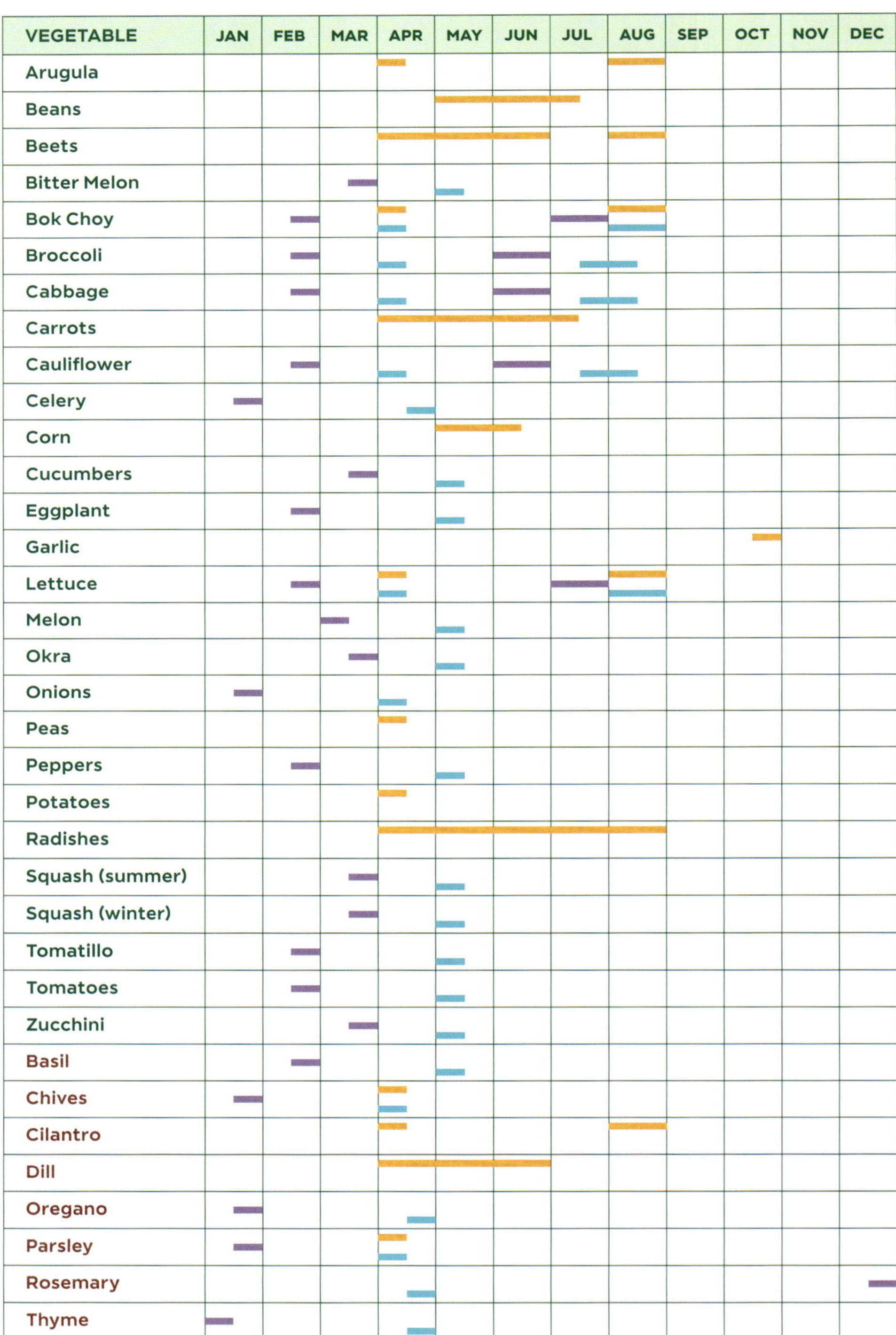

VEGETABLE	JAN	FEB	MAR	APR	MAY	JUN	JUL	AUG	SEP	OCT	NOV	DEC
Arugula				Direct Sow				Direct Sow				
Beans					Direct Sow	Direct Sow	Direct Sow					
Beets				Direct Sow	Direct Sow	Direct Sow	Direct Sow	Direct Sow				
Bitter Melon			Indoor		Transplant							
Bok Choy		Indoor		Direct Sow / Transplant			Indoor	Transplant	Direct Sow			
Broccoli			Indoor	Transplant		Indoor		Transplant				
Cabbage			Indoor	Transplant		Indoor		Transplant				
Carrots				Direct Sow	Direct Sow	Direct Sow	Direct Sow					
Cauliflower			Indoor	Transplant		Indoor		Transplant				
Celery	Indoor			Transplant								
Corn					Direct Sow	Direct Sow						
Cucumbers			Indoor		Transplant							
Eggplant			Indoor		Transplant							
Garlic										Direct Sow		
Lettuce			Indoor	Direct Sow / Transplant			Indoor	Direct Sow / Transplant				
Melon			Indoor									
Okra			Indoor		Transplant							
Onions	Indoor				Transplant							
Peas				Direct Sow								
Peppers			Indoor		Transplant							
Potatoes				Direct Sow								
Radishes				Direct Sow	Direct Sow	Direct Sow	Direct Sow	Direct Sow				
Squash (summer)			Indoor		Transplant							
Squash (winter)			Indoor		Transplant							
Tomatillo			Indoor		Transplant							
Tomatoes			Indoor		Transplant							
Zucchini			Indoor		Transplant							
Basil			Indoor		Transplant							
Chives		Indoor		Direct Sow / Transplant								
Cilantro				Direct Sow				Direct Sow				
Dill				Direct Sow	Direct Sow	Direct Sow						
Oregano		Indoor			Transplant							
Parsley		Indoor		Direct Sow / Transplant								
Rosemary					Transplant							Indoor
Thyme	Indoor				Transplant							

MONTHLY PLANTING SCHEDULE

January
- Planning and seed ordering
- Prepare seed-starting equipment
- **Indoor seed starting (early-January):** thyme
- **Indoor seed starting (mid-January):** celery, onions, chives, oregano, parsley

February
- **Indoor seed starting (mid-February):** bok choy, broccoli, cabbage, cauliflower, lettuce for spring transplants
- **Indoor seed starting (mid-February):** eggplant, peppers, tomatillo, tomatoes, basil for summer transplants

March
- **Indoor seed starting (early-March):** melon
- **Indoor seed starting (mid-March):** bitter melon, cucumber, okra, squash, zucchini

April
- Wait for soil to warm and plant only if soil is workable
- **Direct sow (early-April):** arugula, beets, bok choy, carrots, lettuce, peas, potatoes, radishes, chives, cilantro, dill, parsley
- **Transplant (early-April):** bok choy, broccoli, cabbage, cauliflower, lettuce, chives, parsley, if started indoors
- **Transplant (mid-April):** celery, oregano, rosemary, thyme

May
- **Direct sow (early-May):** beans, corn
- **Transplant (early-May):** all warm-season crops after soil warms

June
- **Indoor seed starting (early-June):** broccoli, cabbage, cauliflower

July
- **Indoor seed starting (early-July):** bok choy, lettuce, for succession planting
- **Transplant (mid-July):** broccoli, cabbage, cauliflower

August
- Begin succession planting for continuous harvest
- **Direct sow (early-August):** arugula, beets, bok choy, lettuce, radishes, cilantro
- **Transplant (early-August):** bok choy, lettuce, if started indoors
- Major harvest period begins

September–November
- Focus: extended harvest with season extension
- **Direct sow (mid-October):** garlic cloves
- Fall garden maintenance

December
- Garden cleanup and planning
- **Indoor seed starting (mid-December):** long-season herbs like rosemary

HIGH DENSITY 4X8 FT GARDEN BED PLAN

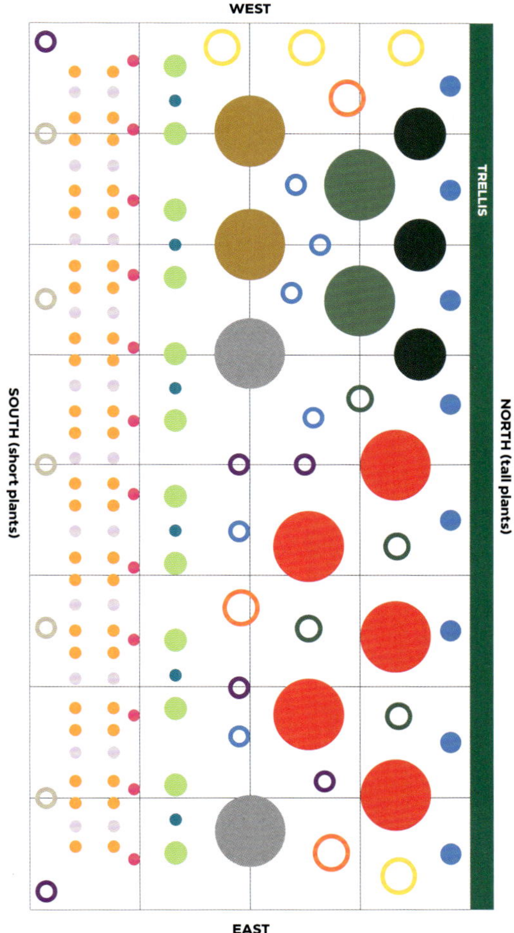

PLANTING SCHEDULE

COOL SEASON
- Beets (22)
- Broccoli (2)
- Cabbage (2)
- Carrots (44)
- Cauliflower (2)
- Chives (6)
- Dill (6)
- Lettuce (12)
- Radishes (12)
- Spinach (6)
- Thyme (5)

WARM SEASON
- Basil (4)
- Cucumbers (3)
- French Marigold (3)
- Nasturtiums (4)
- Pole Beans (8)
- Tomatoes (5)

ZONE 6
(-10°F TO 0°F)
(-23°C TO -18°C)

Growing season:
160–200 days

Last spring frost:
April 1–April 15

First fall frost:
October 15–
November 15

—— Direct Sow

—— Indoor Seed Starting

—— Transplant

Special Considerations

• Excellent balance of growing opportunities

• Good season-extension potential

PLANTING CALENDAR

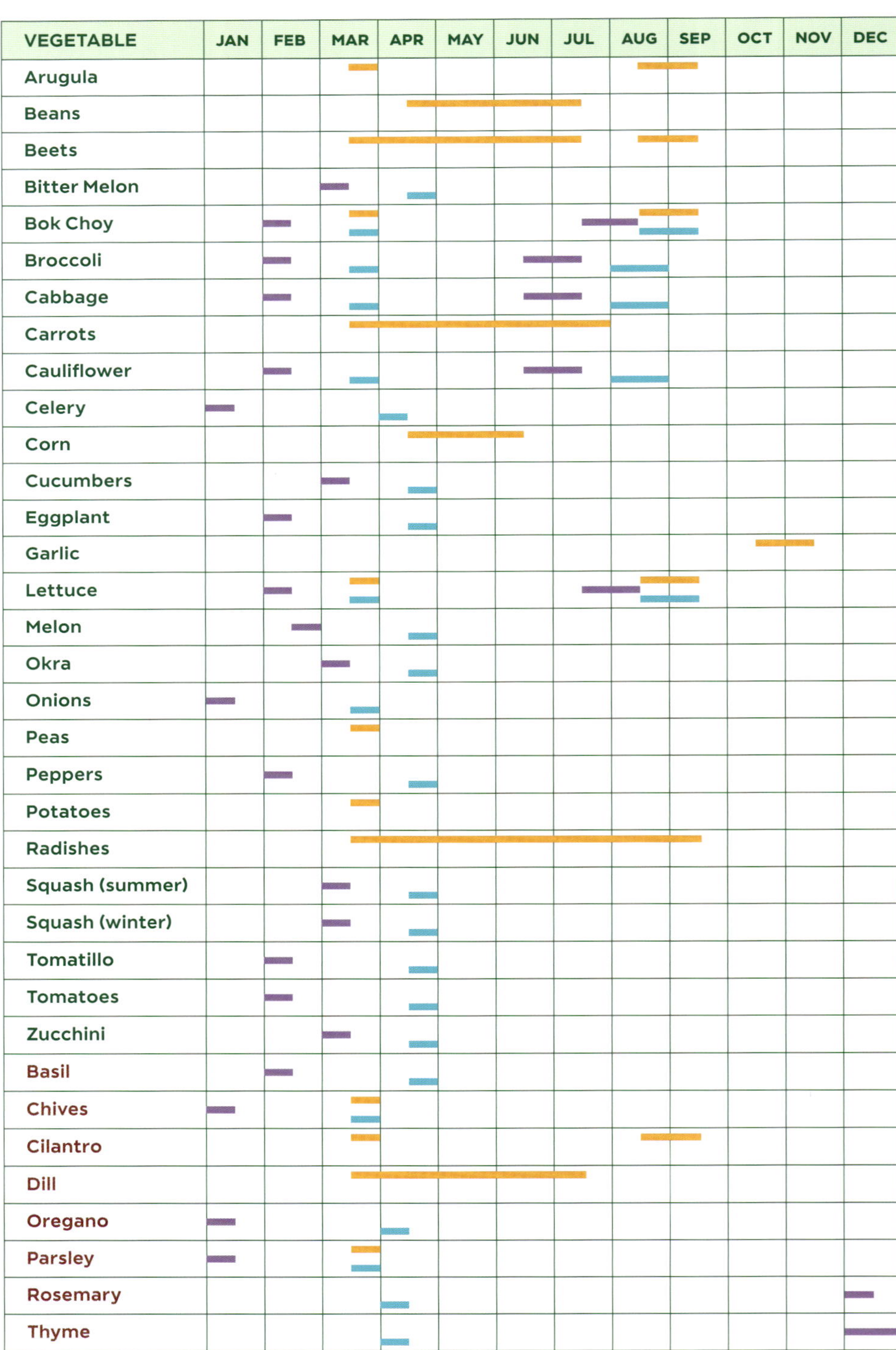

Legend: D = Direct Sow, I = Indoor Seed Starting, T = Transplant

VEGETABLE	JAN	FEB	MAR	APR	MAY	JUN	JUL	AUG	SEP	OCT	NOV	DEC
Arugula			D					D	D			
Beans				D	D	D	D					
Beets			D	D	D	D	D	D	D			
Bitter Melon			I	T								
Bok Choy		I	D/T				I	I/D/T	D/T			
Broccoli		I	T			I	I	T				
Cabbage		I	T			I	I	T	T			
Carrots			D	D	D	D	D					
Cauliflower		I	T			I	I	T				
Celery	I			T								
Corn				D	D							
Cucumbers			I	T								
Eggplant		I		T								
Garlic										D	D	
Lettuce		I	D/T				I	I/D	D/T			
Melon		I	I	T								
Okra			I	T								
Onions	I		T									
Peas			D									
Peppers		I		T								
Potatoes			D									
Radishes			D	D	D	D	D	D				
Squash (summer)			I	T								
Squash (winter)			I	T								
Tomatillo		I		T								
Tomatoes		I		T								
Zucchini			I	T								
Basil		I		T								
Chives	I		D/T									
Cilantro			D					D	D			
Dill			D	D	D	D	D					
Oregano	I			T								
Parsley	I		D/T									
Rosemary				T								I
Thyme				T								I

MONTHLY PLANTING SCHEDULE

January
- Planning and seed ordering
- Prepare seed-starting equipment
- **Indoor seed starting (early-January):** celery, onions, chives, oregano, parsley

February
- **Indoor seed starting (early-February):** bok choy, broccoli, cabbage, cauliflower, lettuce for spring transplants
- **Indoor seed starting (early-February):** eggplant, peppers, tomatillo, tomatoes, basil for summer transplants
- **Indoor seed starting (mid-February):** melon

March
- **Indoor seed starting (early-March):** bitter melon, cucumber, okra, squash, zucchini
- Wait for soil to warm and plant only if soil is workable
- **Direct sow (mid-March):** arugula, beets, bok choy, carrots, lettuce, peas, potatoes, radishes, chives, cilantro, dill, parsley
- **Transplant (mid-March):** bok choy, broccoli, cabbage, cauliflower, lettuce, chives, parsley, if started indoors

April
- **Transplant (early-April):** celery, oregano, rosemary, thyme
- **Direct sow (mid-April):** beans, corn
- **Transplant (mid-April):** all warm-season crops after soil warms

May
- All transplanting completed

June
- **Indoor seed starting (mid-June):** broccoli, cabbage, cauliflower

July
- **Indoor seed starting (mid-July):** bok choy, lettuce for succession planting

August
- Begin succession planting for continuous harvest
- **Transplant (early-August):** broccoli, cabbage, cauliflower
- **Direct sow (mid-August):** arugula, beets, bok choy, lettuce, radishes, cilantro
- **Transplant (mid-August):** bok choy, lettuce, if started indoors

September
- Extend growing season preparations
- **Final plantings of quick crops (early-September):** arugula, bok choy, lettuce, radishes, cilantro

October–November
- Extended harvest with protection
- **Direct sow (late-October):** garlic cloves
- Begin garden cleanup

December
- Garden cleanup and planning
- **Indoor seed starting (early-December):** long-season herbs like rosemary and thyme

HIGH DENSITY 4X8 FT GARDEN BED PLAN

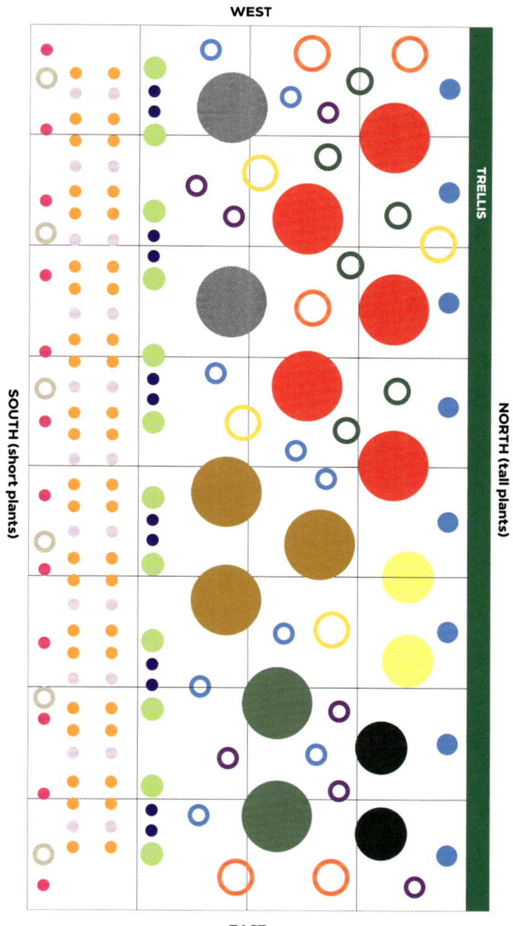

PLANTING SCHEDULE

COOL SEASON
- Arugula (12)
- Broccoli (2)
- Brussels Sprouts (2)
- Carrots (44)
- Cauliflower (2)
- Chives (7)
- Dill (9)
- Lettuce (12)
- Onions (22)
- Parsley (6)
- Radishes (12)

WARM SEASON
- Basil (6)
- French Marigold (5)
- Peppers (2)
- Pole Beans (8)
- Squash (3)
- Tomatoes (5)
- Zinnias (4)

ZONE 7
(0°F TO 10°F)
(−18°C TO −12°C)

Growing season:
180–220 days

Last spring frost:
March 15–April 15

First fall frost:
November 1–
November 30

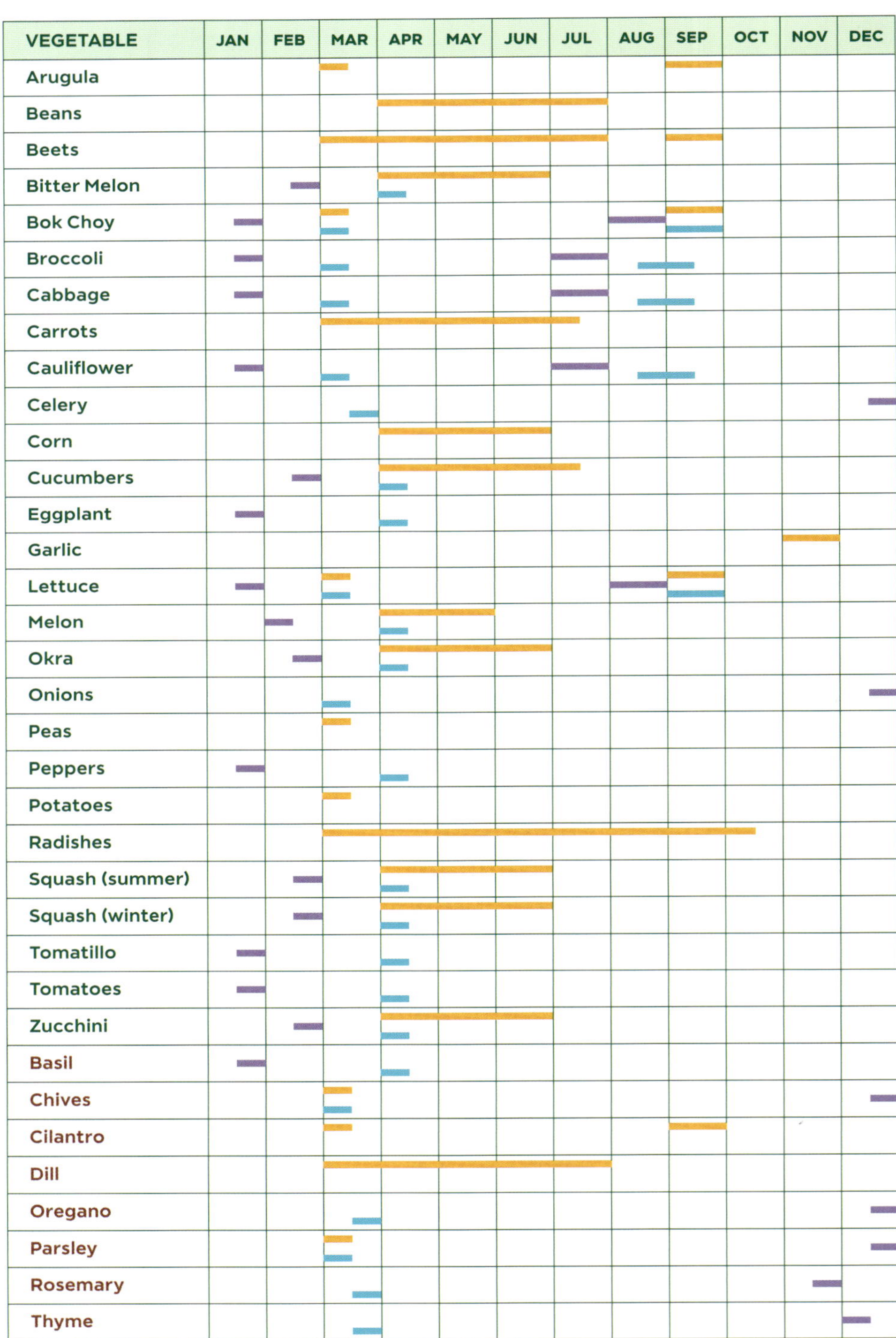

Direct Sow

Indoor Seed Starting

Transplant

Special Considerations

• Summer heat requires protection for sensitive crops

• Excellent fall growing opportunities

PLANTING CALENDAR

Legend: **D** = Direct Sow · **I** = Indoor Seed Starting · **T** = Transplant

VEGETABLE	JAN	FEB	MAR	APR	MAY	JUN	JUL	AUG	SEP	OCT	NOV	DEC
Arugula			D						D			
Beans				D	D	D	D					
Beets			D	D	D	D	D	D	D			
Bitter Melon		I	I	T								
Bok Choy	I		D/T					I	D/T			
Broccoli	I		T				I		T			
Cabbage	I		T				I	T				
Carrots			D	D	D	D	D					
Cauliflower	I		T				I					
Celery				T								I
Corn				D	D	D	D					
Cucumbers		I	I	D/T	D	D	D					
Eggplant	I			T								
Garlic											D	
Lettuce	I		D/T					I	D/T			
Melon		I		D/T	D							
Okra			I	D/T	D	D	D					
Onions			T									I
Peas			D									
Peppers	I			T								
Potatoes			D									
Radishes			D	D	D	D	D	D				
Squash (summer)			I	D/T	D	D						
Squash (winter)			I	D/T	D	D						
Tomatillo	I											
Tomatoes	I											
Zucchini			I	D/T	D	D						
Basil	I					T						
Chives			D/T									I
Cilantro									D			
Dill			D	D	D	D	D					
Oregano			T									I
Parsley			D/T									I
Rosemary			T								I	
Thyme			T									I

MONTHLY PLANTING SCHEDULE

January
- Planning and seed ordering
- Prepare seed-starting equipment
- **Indoor seed starting (mid-January):** bok choy, broccoli, cabbage, cauliflower, lettuce for spring transplants
- **Indoor seed starting (mid-January):** eggplant, peppers, tomatillo, tomatoes, basil for summer transplants

February
- **Indoor seed starting (early-February):** melon
- **Indoor seed starting (mid-February):** bitter melon, cucumber, okra, squash, zucchini

March
- Wait for soil to warm and plant only if soil is workable
- **Direct sow (early-March):** arugula, beets, bok choy, carrots, lettuce, peas, potatoes, radishes, chives, cilantro, dill, parsley
- **Transplant (early-March):** bok choy, broccoli, cabbage, cauliflower, lettuce, chives, parsley, if started indoors
- **Transplant (mid-March):** celery, oregano, rosemary, thyme

April
- **Direct sow (early-April):** beans, corn
- **Transplant (early-April):** all warm-season crops after soil warms

May
- Succession planting
- Prepare for summer heat

June
- Heat protection setup for sensitive crops
- Continue succession planting
- Plan fall garden

July
- **Indoor seed starting (early-July):** broccoli, cabbage, cauliflower

August
- **Indoor seed starting (early-August):** bok choy, lettuce
- **Transplant (mid-August):** broccoli, cabbage, cauliflower

September
- Major fall planting period
- **Direct sow (early-September):** arugula, beets, bok choy, lettuce, radishes, cilantro
- **Transplant (early-September):** bok choy, lettuce, if started indoors
- Extend growing season preparations
- **Final plantings of quick crops (early-September):** arugula, bok choy, lettuce, radishes, cilantro

October
- Extend season preparations

November
- **Direct sow (early-November):** garlic cloves
- **Indoor seed starting (mid-November):** long-season herbs like rosemary and thyme
- Begin garden cleanup

December
- Garden planning for next season
- **Indoor seed starting (mid-December):** celery, onions, chives, oregano, parsley

HIGH DENSITY 4X8 FT GARDEN BED PLAN

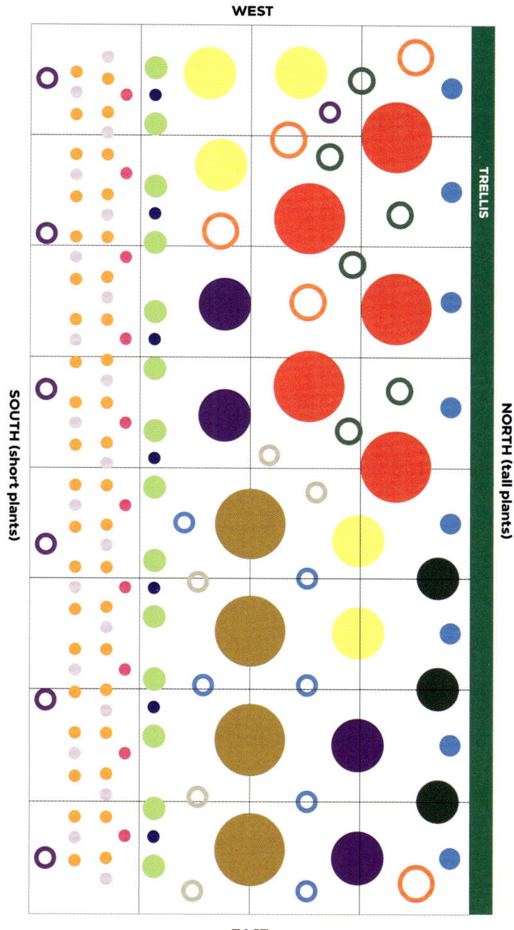

PLANTING SCHEDULE

COOL SEASON	WARM SEASON
Arugula (7)	Basil (6)
Beets (21)	Cucumbers (3)
Carrots (40)	Eggplant (4)
Chives (7)	French Marigold (5)
Lettuce (14)	Peppers (5)
Oregano (6)	Pole Beans (8)
Parsley (5)	Tomatoes (5)
Radishes (10)	Zucchini (4)

ZONE 8
(10°F TO 20°F)
(-12°C TO -7°C)

Growing season:

200–250 days

Last spring frost:

March 1–March 30

First fall frost:

November 15–
December 15

___ **Direct Sow**

___ **Indoor Seed Starting**

___ **Transplant**

Special Considerations

• Summer heat limits planting significantly

• Excellent fall/winter growing opportunities

• Heat protection essential in summer

PLANTING CALENDAR

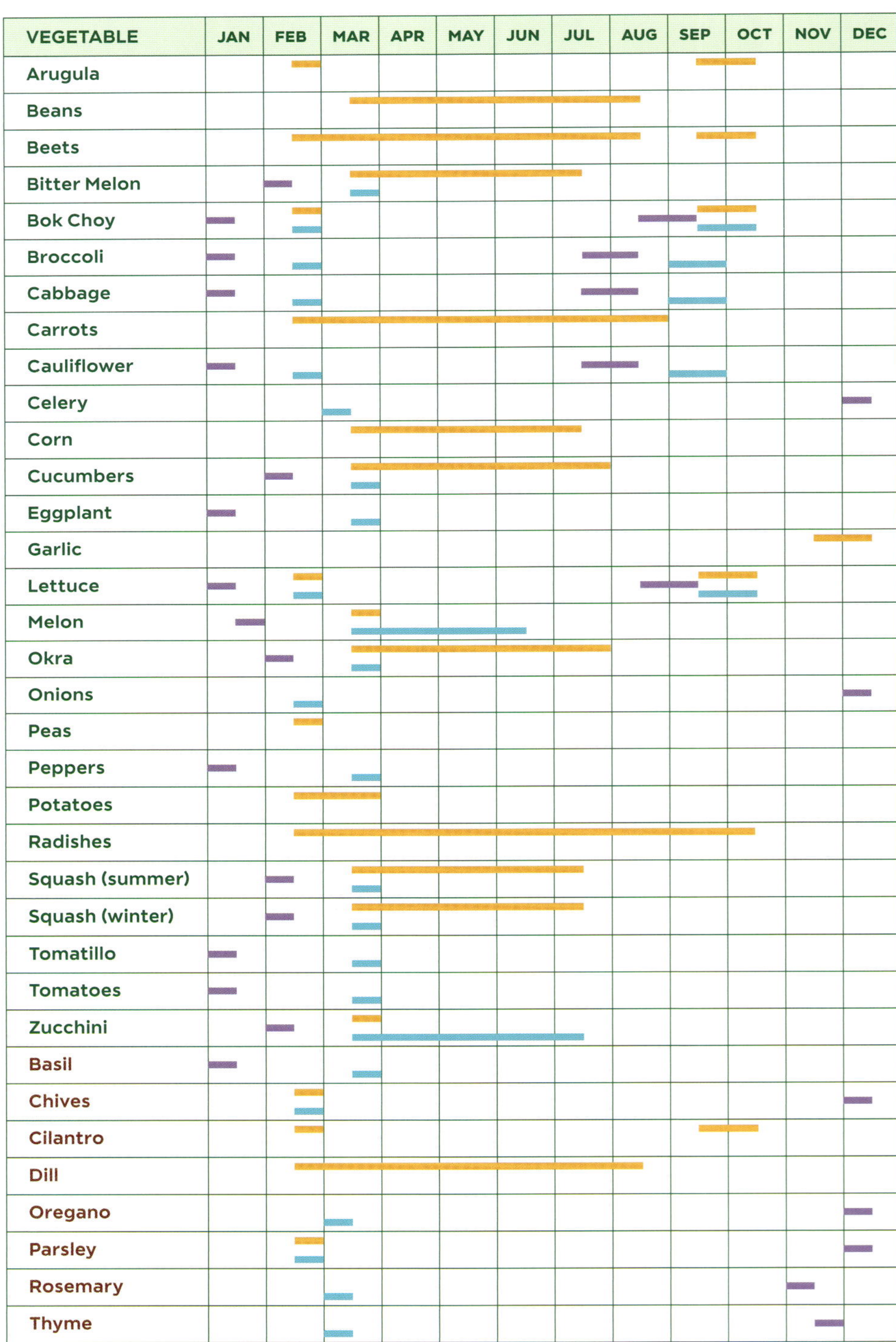

MONTHLY PLANTING SCHEDULE

January
- **Indoor seed starting (early-January):** bok choy, broccoli, cabbage, cauliflower, lettuce for spring transplants
- **Indoor seed starting (early-January):** eggplant, peppers, tomatillo, tomatoes, basil for summer transplants
- **Indoor seed starting (mid-January):** melon

February
- **Indoor seed starting (early-February):** bitter melon, cucumber, okra, squash, zucchini
- **Direct sow (mid-February):** arugula, beets, bok choy, carrots, lettuce, peas, potatoes, radishes, chives, cilantro, dill, parsley
- **Transplant (mid-February):** bok choy, broccoli, cabbage, cauliflower, lettuce, chives, parsley, if started indoors

March
- **Transplant (early-March):** celery, oregano, rosemary, thyme
- **Direct sow (mid-March):** beans, corn
- **Transplant (mid-March):** all warm-season crops

April
- Final cool-season plantings before heat

May
- Focus on heat-tolerant crops only
- Succession plant heat-tolerant varieties

June-July
- Limited planting due to extreme heat
- Focus on maintenance and harvest
- **Indoor seed starting (mid-July):** broccoli, cabbage, cauliflower

August
- Begin fall planting preparation
- **Indoor seed starting (mid-August):** bok choy, lettuce

September
- **Transplant (early-September):** broccoli, cabbage, cauliflower
- **Direct sow (mid-September):** arugula, beets, bok choy, lettuce, radishes, cilantro
- **Transplant (mid-September):** bok choy, lettuce, if started indoors

October
- Cool-season crop focus

November
- **Direct sow (mid-November):** garlic cloves
- **Indoor seed starting (mid-November):** long-season herbs like rosemary and thyme

December
- **Indoor seed starting (mid-December):** celery, onions, chives, oregano, parsley

HIGH DENSITY 4X8 FT GARDEN BED PLAN

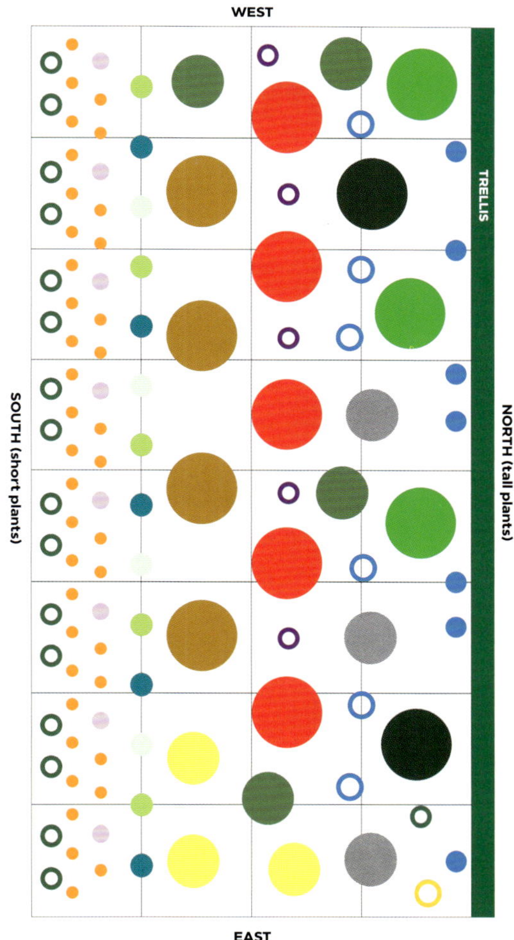

PLANTING SCHEDULE

COOL SEASON
- Bok Choy (5)
- Carrots (39)
- Green Onions (16)
- Lettuce (5)
- Mizuna (4)
- Turnips (8)

WARM SEASON
- Armenian Cucumber (3)
- Bell Peppers (3)
- Cantaloupe (3)
- Cilantro (5)
- Nasturtium (1)
- Okra (4)
- Pole Beans (7)
- Sumer Squash (4)
- Thai Basil (6)
- Tomatoes (5)
- Watermelon (2)

ZONE 9
(20°F TO 30°F)
(-7°C TO -1°C)

Growing season:

250–300 days

Last spring frost:

February 15–
March 15

First fall frost:

December 1–
December 31

— Direct Sow

— Indoor Seed Starting

— Transplant

Special Considerations

• Summer heat severely limits planting options

• Excellent fall/winter/spring growing

• Focus on heat-tolerant varieties for limited summer crops

PLANTING CALENDAR

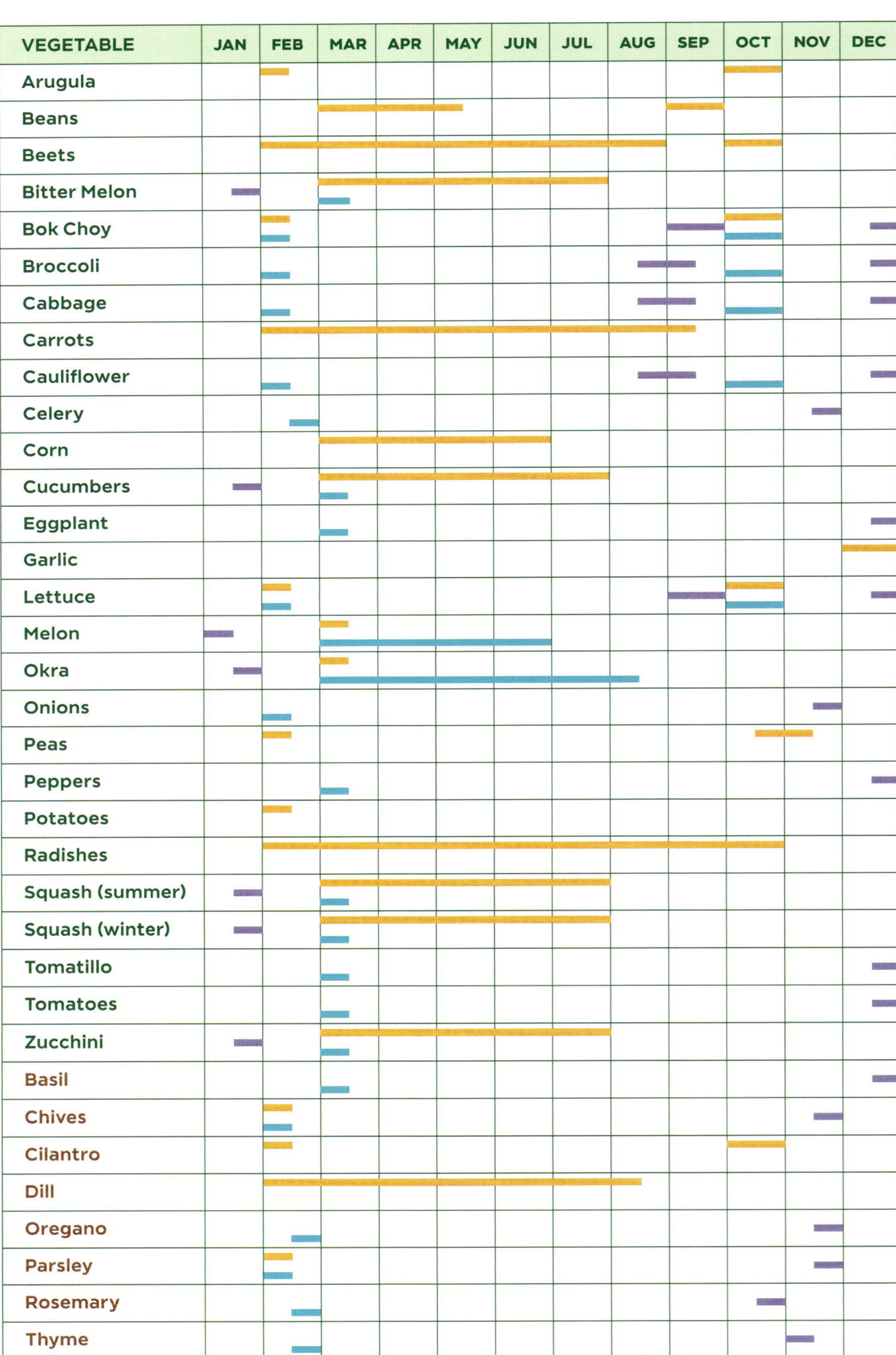

VEGETABLE	JAN	FEB	MAR	APR	MAY	JUN	JUL	AUG	SEP	OCT	NOV	DEC
Arugula		Direct Sow								Direct Sow		
Beans			Direct Sow	Direct Sow					Direct Sow			
Beets		Direct Sow	Direct Sow	Direct Sow	Direct Sow	Direct Sow				Direct Sow		
Bitter Melon	Indoor		Transplant									
Bok Choy		Direct Sow / Transplant							Indoor	Direct Sow / Transplant		Indoor
Broccoli		Direct Sow						Indoor	Indoor			Indoor
Cabbage		Transplant						Indoor		Transplant		Indoor
Carrots		Direct Sow	Direct Sow	Direct Sow	Direct Sow	Direct Sow	Direct Sow					
Cauliflower		Transplant						Indoor				Indoor
Celery			Transplant								Indoor	
Corn			Direct Sow	Direct Sow	Direct Sow							
Cucumbers	Indoor		Direct Sow / Transplant	Direct Sow	Direct Sow							
Eggplant				Transplant								Indoor
Garlic												Direct Sow
Lettuce		Direct Sow / Transplant							Indoor	Direct Sow		Indoor
Melon	Indoor		Transplant	Transplant	Transplant	Transplant						
Okra		Indoor	Direct Sow	Transplant	Transplant	Transplant	Transplant					
Onions		Transplant									Indoor	
Peas		Direct Sow								Direct Sow		
Peppers			Transplant									Indoor
Potatoes		Direct Sow										
Radishes		Direct Sow	Direct Sow	Direct Sow	Direct Sow	Direct Sow	Direct Sow	Direct Sow	Direct Sow			
Squash (summer)	Indoor		Direct Sow / Transplant									
Squash (winter)	Indoor		Direct Sow	Transplant								
Tomatillo			Transplant									Indoor
Tomatoes			Transplant									Indoor
Zucchini	Indoor		Transplant									
Basil												Indoor
Chives		Direct Sow / Transplant									Indoor	
Cilantro		Direct Sow								Direct Sow		
Dill		Direct Sow	Direct Sow	Direct Sow	Direct Sow	Direct Sow	Direct Sow					
Oregano		Transplant									Indoor	
Parsley		Direct Sow / Transplant									Indoor	
Rosemary			Transplant							Indoor		
Thyme			Transplant								Indoor	

MONTHLY PLANTING SCHEDULE

January
- **Indoor seed starting (mid-January):** melon
- **Indoor seed starting (mid-January):** bitter melon, cucumber, okra, squash, zucchini

February
- **Direct sow (early-February):** arugula, beets, bok choy, carrots, lettuce, peas, potatoes, radishes, chives, cilantro, dill, parsley
- **Transplant (early-February):** bok choy, broccoli, cabbage, cauliflower, lettuce, chives, parsley, if started indoors
- **Transplant (mid-February):** celery, oregano, rosemary, thyme

March
- **Direct sow (early-March):** beans, corn
- **Transplant (early-March):** all warm-season crops

April-May
- Limited warm-season plantings
- Focus on heat-tolerant varieties only
- Succession plant carefully

June-July
- Very limited planting due to extreme heat
- Focus on harvest and maintenance

August
- Prepare fall garden extensively
- **Indoor seed starting (mid-August):** broccoli, cabbage, cauliflower

September
- **Indoor seed starting (early-September):** bok choy, lettuce

October
- **Transplant (early-October):** broccoli, cabbage, cauliflower, bok choy, lettuce, if started indoors
- **Direct sow (early-October):** arugula, beets, bok choy, lettuce, radishes, cilantro
- **Direct sow (mid-October):** peas
- **Indoor seed starting (mid-October):** long-season herbs like rosemary and thyme

November
- **Indoor seed starting (mid-November):** celery, onions, chives, oregano, parsley

December
- **Direct sow (early-December):** garlic cloves
- **Indoor seed starting (mid-December):** bok choy, broccoli, cabbage, cauliflower, lettuce for spring transplants
- **Indoor seed starting (mid-December):** eggplant, peppers, tomatillo, tomatoes, basil for summer transplants

HIGH DENSITY 4X8 FT GARDEN BED PLAN

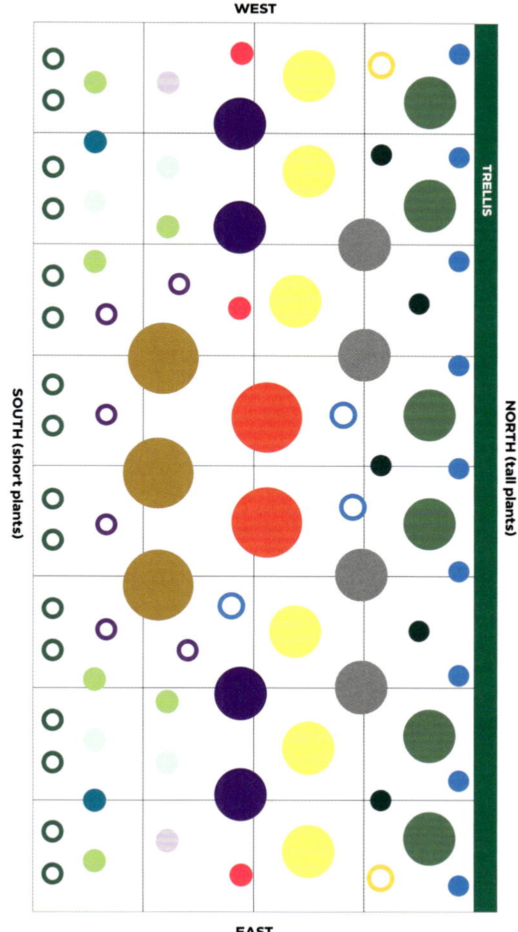

PLANTING SCHEDULE

COOL SEASON
- Armenian Cucumber (4)
- Bok Choy (2)
- Cilantro (6)
- Collard Greens (2)
- Green Onions (16)
- Lemongrass (2)
- Lettuce (6)
- Mustard Greens (4)
- Okra (6)
- Rainbow Chard (3)
- Southern Peas (5)
- Thai Basil (3)

WARM SEASON
- Peppers (6)
- Summer Squash (3)
- Tomatoes (2)
- Yard Long Beans (9)

ZONE 10
(30°F TO 40°F)
(−1°C TO 4°C)

Growing season:

300+ days

Last spring frost:

January 30–

February 28

First fall frost:

December 15–

January 15 (rare)

Direct Sow

Indoor Seed Starting

Transplant

Special Considerations

• Summer heat makes most planting impossible

• Excellent cool-season growing (fall/winter/spring)

• Requires heat-tolerant varieties for limited summer production

• Season extension and shade crucial for summer crops

PLANTING CALENDAR

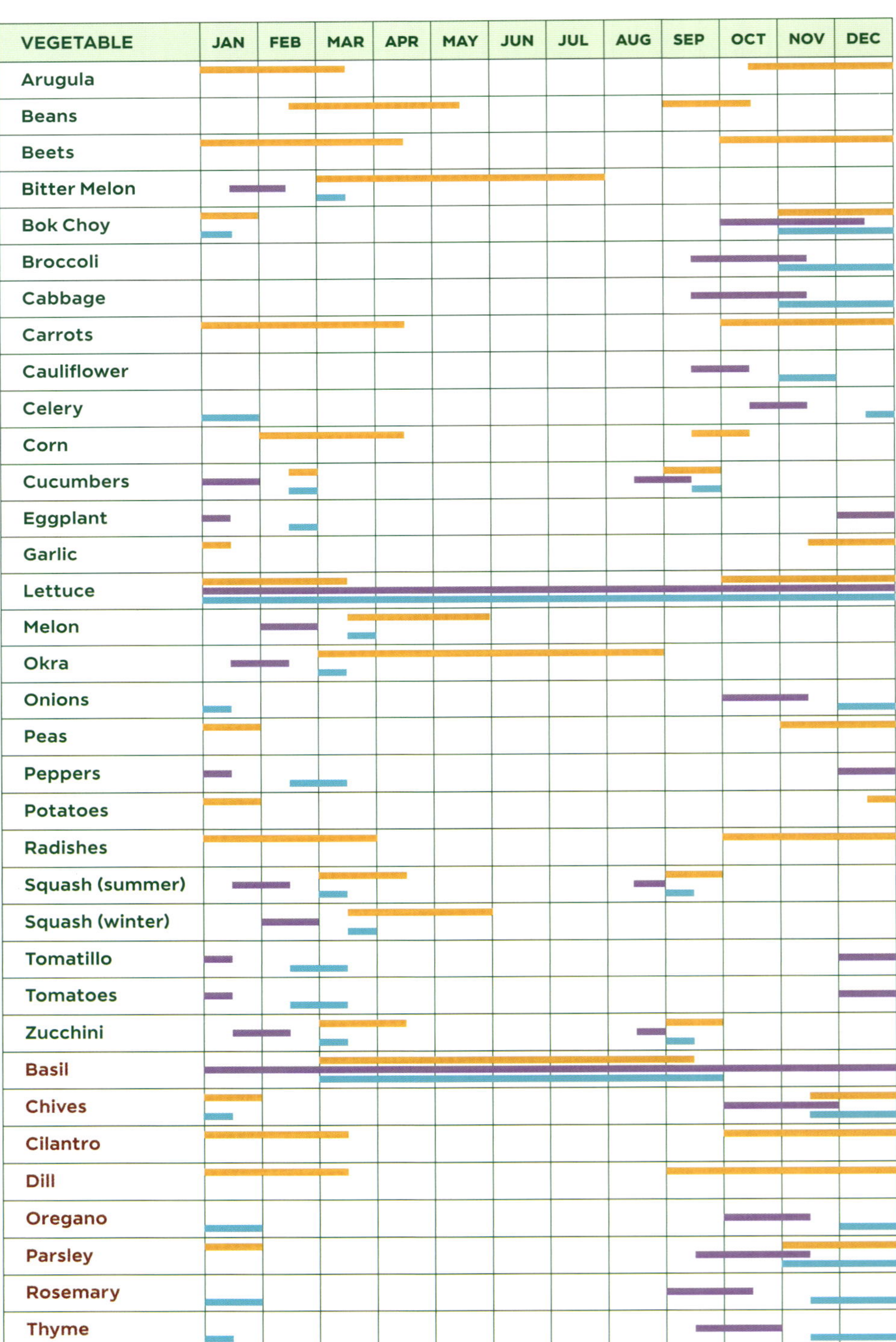

MONTHLY PLANTING SCHEDULE

January
- **Direct sow:** cool-season crops, peas
- **Indoor seed starting:** heat-sensitive summer crops

February
- Continue cool-season plantings
- Begin warm-season crop preparation
- **Transplant:** early warm-season crops

March
- **Direct sow:** early warm-season crops
- Focus on crops that tolerate some heat
- Final cool-season plantings

April–May
- Very limited planting options
- Only extremely heat-tolerant varieties
- Focus on maintenance

June–August
- Minimal planting due to extreme heat
- Focus on harvest of heat-tolerant crops
- Extensive fall preparation

September
- Resume normal planting schedule
- Major fall planting begins
- Cool-season crop focus

October
- Continue fall plantings
- Full planting schedule resumed

November
- Cool-season succession planting
- Winter crop establishment

December
- Continue cool-season plantings
- Year-round garden maintenance

HIGH DENSITY 4X8 FT GARDEN BED PLAN

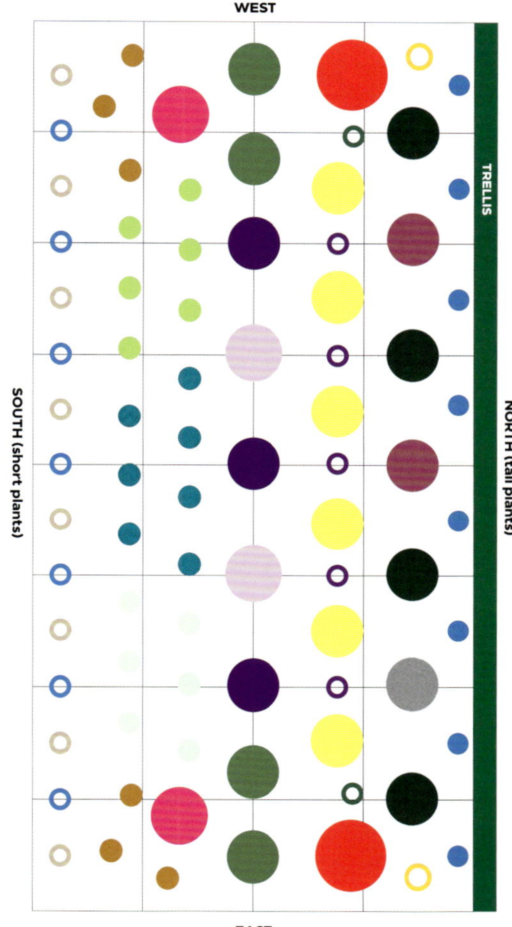

PLANTING SCHEDULE

COOL SEASON
- Amaranth (2)
- Bittermelon (4)
- Bok Choy (6)
- Cilantro (5)
- Culantro (7)
- Gai Lan (7)
- Heat-Tolerant Lettuce (6)
- Lemongrass (2)
- Okra (4)
- Shiso Perilla (8)
- Thai Basil (2)
- Water Spinach (6)

WARM SEASON
- Chayote (1)
- Eggplant (3)
- Luffa (2)
- Peppers (6)
- Tomatillos (2)
- Tomatoes (2)
- Yard Long Beans (8)

SUCCESSION PLANTING, INTERPLANTING, AND SHADE GROWING

SUCCESSION PLANTING TIMING STRATEGIES

This technique maximizes productivity and ensures a continuous supply of fresh vegetables from spring through fall.

- **Weekly plantings (every 7–10 days):** Fast growers such as lettuce, arugula, radishes, spinach, and cilantro
- **Biweekly plantings (every 2 weeks):** Bush beans, snap peas, carrots, beets, and summer squash
- **Monthly plantings (every 3–4 weeks):** Broccoli, cabbage, kale, cauliflower, and Brussels sprouts

INTERPLANTING WINNING COMBINATIONS

Interplanting involves combining crops with different growth rates, root depths, or harvest times in the same bed to achieve multiple harvests from one space. Plant fast-maturing crops between slower-growing ones.

Winning combinations:

- **Lettuce + Tomatoes + Basil:** Lettuce fills ground space and is harvested before tomatoes expand; basil grows throughout the season.
- **Radishes + Carrots + Onions:** Radishes break up soil and mature quickly; onions deter carrot flies while growing at different depths.
- **Bush Beans + Cucumbers + Radishes:** Beans fix nitrogen, cucumbers climb above, and radishes are harvested first.

- **Beets + Broccoli + Lettuce:** Ground-level beets and lettuce grow beneath towering broccoli.
- **Peppers + Basil + Chives:** Vertical peppers, mid-level basil, and aphid-deterring chives at ground level.

BEST SHADE VEGETABLES

Partial shade (3–4 hours of direct sun or dappled light) can still produce abundant harvests with proper plant selection.

- **Lettuce & Spinach:** Very shade-tolerant; produce tender, sweet leaves with less bolting.
- **Kale & Arugula:** Hardy greens that develop a sweeter, less bitter flavor in lower light.
- **Bok Choy & Asian Greens:** Naturally shade-tolerant with mild flavor.
- **Radishes & Beets:** Fast-growing roots; beets also produce excellent greens even when roots are smaller.
- **Parsley & Cilantro:** Prefer shade protection and are less prone to bolting.
- **Success Tips:** Shade vegetables grow more slowly and yield less than full-sun crops. Compensate by enriching soil with compost, maintaining consistent moisture, and allowing longer growing periods.

ACKNOWLEDGMENTS

First and foremost, we're deeply grateful for the incredible community that's grown around @plantedinthegarden. Watching so many of you discover the joy of gardening has meant the world to us and inspired every page of this book.

To our parents: A million thank-yous wouldn't be enough. Every sacrifice you made and all the support you've given us created the foundation for everything we do today. We are forever grateful.

To our son: Thank you for being part of this journey with us every step of the way—from seedling to harvest, through every season. We're so grateful for you, and we can't wait to see your future bloom as beautifully as your garden will.

A heartfelt thank-you to everyone at DK and Penguin Random House—especially Alexander Rigby and Joanna Price—for your expertise, guidance, and hard work in helping bring this book to life. Thank you to Claire Baldwin for capturing our garden so beautifully through your illustrations.

Finally, to everyone with a small space: This book is for you. We've learned that gardening isn't about the size of your space—it's about making the most of what you have. Your compact garden holds limitless potential, just like you do.

INDEX

ABOUT THE AUTHORS

Char and Marv Lopez are urban gardeners on a simple mission: get as many people as possible to grow their own food. They created a successful online community with over 6 million followers who turn to them for practical DIY solutions and small-space gardening hacks. They call Toronto home, where they tend their garden with their son—designing it to work with nature, building soil health and biodiversity, while still discovering something new with every season.